THE WISER DIVORCE

THE
WISER
DIVORCE

POSITIVE STRATEGIES FOR
YOUR **NEXT** BEST LIFE

ANGIE HALLIER

MEGÈVE PRESS

Megève Press LLC

Copyright © 2014 by Angie Hallier

ISBN: 978-0-692-25838-5

Digital editions available.

Manufactured in the United States of America
First Edition

www.AngieHallier.com

To
Tiffany,
Gerard
and Gene—
My triumvirate
of
laughs,
love
and strength.

Table of Contents

START YOUR TRANSITION WITH THE WISER DIVORCE

There are things about divorce you cannot possibly know if you are not a divorce attorney or involved in the divorce industry—things your divorce attorney, friends, or family might never tell you or even know to tell you. Things that could make a profound difference in your life, both during and after your divorce.

That is why I wrote this book. After decades of being a divorce attorney, I have seen firsthand how divorces can go terribly wrong and how they can go surprisingly right. I know how people's words, attitudes and behaviors can impact the divorce process itself and their lives after divorce. I wrote this book to help people going through divorce learn these truths.

"The Wiser Divorce" is about strategies, from how to talk to your children about divorce, to finding the right attorney, to how to keep judges and courts from controlling too much of your destiny. It will help you focus on the emotional changes you'll make during your divorce and how those changes impact both short-term results and the long-term outcome. It is about strategically controlling how you think, talk and act about your divorce in order to achieve the optimal outcome for you at the end of the legal process of divorce and for the rest of your life.

Engaging in the Wiser Divorce can also *reshape* who you are by leading you to your Next Best Life. This life transition can become your opportunity to transform yourself and your future. It can become a way to heal a family that is broken. It can free you to discover the best life that awaits you. That is the focus of this book: Becoming wise about your approach to divorce so that it becomes your pathway to a new life.

You can begin to surrender your old life, and start to heal, by focusing your thoughts, your words and your actions on your new life—but not just any life: Your Next Best Life.

As you navigate the life transition of a divorce, a transition that too often becomes traumatic and destructive, I hope you'll find this book to be your manual for how to move forward positively and with hope.

1   Wise Up About Your Divorce

The definition of divorce is simple enough: It's the legal process of ending a marriage.

But when we apply it to our own lives, divorce becomes anything but simple or clear. If you're reading this book, you may be experiencing that first-hand.

Divorce is a life crisis. The dreams you had for your life when you said "I do" are gone. The person you thought you married isn't the person you are married to any longer. And nothing seems "for sure" anymore.

Even if you are the one who first brought up the "D" word, the emotions attached to divorce can be complex, frightening, and painful. Inevitably these emotions seem to become part of the process.

But do these emotions have to rule your divorce and drive you to madness? No. There is another way.

Can divorce focus more on process and less on emotions? Yes. It can.

Is there a way to approach divorce that can turn your divorce into a strategic gateway to a better future? There is.

It's the wiser way to divorce. And this book offers you the tools to get strategic, to think wisely about your options and your interactions, and to get on with your Next Best Life.

GETTING STUCK IN THE UGLINESS

We've all seen how divorce most often plays out. Whether it's your friends, your neighbors, your siblings, or your parents, you've most likely seen someone in the middle of an ugly divorce. Unhappy couples reach their limit; then anger and fear set in. People say and do things that hurt, and soon their divorce becomes as miserable as their marriage.

The ugliness can go on for months, or years, sometimes even long after the papers have been signed and the divorce is final. Some people get stuck in the ugliness of their divorce and spend the rest of their lives hauling around that baggage of anger and fear … shame and spite … and worst of all, victimhood.

If you are reading this book because divorce is now or may soon be part of your own reality, you are probably wishing you could just snap your fingers and make it go away.

That's why I wrote this book: to show you how it's possible to minimize the hostility in your divorce.

It may not happen quickly, and it may not always be easy, but I can help you transform the way you speak, act, and think during the divorce process to get past a lot of the negativity. I will show you how to get strategic about your divorce. I will show you how to start focusing on the goals you have for your Next Best Life.

Positive, strategic, and focused on the future: That's the Wiser Divorce.

DIVORCE AS A BATTLEGROUND

In too many divorces, the drama gets cranked up so high the entire process looks and sounds like a battleground. People (or their attorneys) pull out their deadliest weapons—threats, accusations, intimidation, rage, and shrieking voices. People get battered and bloody; the most wounded are almost always the children. In these cases divorce is war. In a war, somebody's going to win, and somebody's going to lose, or at least that is what people expect. However, in a war, even the winners rarely come out unscathed.

There's nothing wise or strategic about a divorce that looks like that.

Yet most people don't question this adversarial model for divorcing a spouse. It's always been that way.

Why is it that way? Why does a model that doesn't really work for anyone continue to be the way things get done?

We could find plenty of complex answers to that question. Gender inequality made divorce an economic disaster for women and children for centuries, setting the stage for a battleground over money and property. Society's rigid standards for morality ratcheted up the element of shame. For many years divorce was such a taboo that many people resorted to the only way they could imagine being happy—having an affair.

With children and money and pride and moral rectitude at stake, is it any wonder divorce became a high-stakes battleground?

This battleground mentality colors the way people react to divorce—and not just to their own divorce. You have probably seen what can happen when friends and family line up on the side of the person they think is "in the right" and start condemning the person they think is "in the wrong."

But divorce is different today. Right? The laws protect children. Women have economic power. No-fault divorce, which started to become standard practice in the 1970s, allowed people to divorce without accusing a spouse of adultery or abuse. Today, even churches are full of people with ex-spouses, so divorce doesn't cast people into some moral purgatory any more. Yet the battleground mentality still persists. Why?

Because even the legal process itself is still designed to make divorce a battleground. Existing divorce law in the United States says *the only way to end your marriage is for one party to file a lawsuit against the other.*

That's right. If you want to get out of a marriage that is making you miserable or wrecking your life or placing your children in the crossfire, you have to sue the person who has shared your bed, trusted you with life's deepest secrets, and maybe even made babies with you. Divorce, by law, starts as an adversarial act. File a lawsuit. With that as the starting point, it's easy to think the only outcome is: you will win, or you will lose. Does that sound wise to you?

The truth is that the courts still have a great deal of control over divorce. And that keeps the process adversarial.

Top 10 Emotionally Healthy Reasons Clients File for Divorce

1. Abuse is occurring, be it hands-on physical abuse, threats, intimidation, isolation, or other emotional abuse.

2. Children are being affected by the conflict.

3. Counseling hasn't helped.

4. A mental disorder or unacknowledged drug or alcohol abuse is involved.

5. The only reason to stay is "for the children."

6. The family is headed toward financial ruin if a spouse doesn't stop doing whatever he or she is doing.

7. Depression or anxiety from the bad marriage is seriously affecting the whole family.

8. Unhappiness in the marriage is such that anywhere is better than being at home.

9. A betrayal has occurred of such magnitude that trust cannot be restored.

10. Goals in life or for children simply cannot be realized by staying in the marriage.

Think about it. When we get married, we're altering our future significantly. We're entering into a legal arrangement that is going to impact every part of our lives, from our individual autonomy to where we live to our personal economics. Yet we don't have to ask a judge to approve our plans, do we? All we have to do to enter into this legal agreement is to get a license. The courts don't tell us we can't get married in a Lutheran church, or require us to have our father walk us down the aisle, or put the seal of approval on our decision to have children right away or not at all.

When it comes to getting married, the law treats us like the grown-ups we are and trusts us to figure it out.

When it comes to the decision to divorce, however, the courts traditionally have had the final say. The courts determine the details that will impact almost every aspect of our future lives. How much money we'll walk away with. Who will get the house, the car and the family silver. Where the children will live and where they'll spend their holidays.

Around the country, states are legalizing same-sex marriages. I can assure you, every principle in this book can and will apply to same-sex divorces. Because, as surely as LGBT couples fall in love and make a commitment, there will be times when those vows break down and somebody wants out.

Our legal system was set up to address wrongs. It deals with criminals. It decides who's in the wrong when there's a car wreck, or whether someone is guilty of medical malpractice when healthcare goes awry. When divorce laws were first written, somebody had to be in the wrong before a divorce could be granted. Somebody had to be cheating or abusing or otherwise be some kind of evil scoundrel before the other person—who was presumed to be the innocent victim—could file a lawsuit to be released from their marital hell.

So historically divorce, like most other legal proceedings, addressed a wrong. Today, the litigation model of divorce still stands, despite the fact that no-fault divorce is the norm.

Today, no one has to be a cheating, abusing, evil scoundrel in order for a couple to be granted a divorce. People who are unhappy can decide to put their marriage out of its misery. However, for the most part, the legal system, families, communities, and society still tend to treat the act of ending a marriage like something to be won or lost.

This adversarial system helps no one in the end.

Viewing divorce as purely an adversarial action rarely leads to the healthiest, happiest, or wisest outcome. It's certainly not the ideal way to launch your Next Best Life. And isn't that what we all ultimately hope for when we go through a divorce? Our Next Best Life?

Divorce as a legal battleground needs to stop because it creates too much trauma. It beats people down. And, frankly, it costs way too much money. *Your* money. Money you could use to put your kids through college or rebuild your own life.

So what do we do? How do we get to a different outcome? How do we shift from a divorce that creates wreckage to the Wiser Divorce?

A DECISION TO BE HAPPY

The people who are in the best position to change the way their divorce plays out are people who are willing to look at divorce differently while they are walking through it. People going through a divorce can change not only the way *they* view and experience divorce and the way *they* themselves will emerge from the divorce; they also have the ability to affect the way their friends, family, and children experience their divorce. And this can ultimately change the way society views divorce.

In the Wiser Divorce, ending a marriage is viewed as a turning point, one of life's many transitions. A way to shift out of unhappiness and into happiness. A change of life status to be realized leaving your hopes and dreams—and dignity—still intact.

Suppose for a moment that you cannot find a way to be happy in your present marriage. Now imagine posting a question to your friends on Facebook: Do you want me to be happy or unhappy? Most people, answering from their hearts, would of course vote for you to be happy.

That's what divorce is and can be—a decision to be happy. A decision to change something in your life that is no longer working.

Divorce is a way to reset your life path, and resetting your path doesn't have to be bad. We all reset our paths many times in life. We move. We change careers or accept a promotion. We decide to have children. We lose 40 pounds and run a marathon. We learn to walk again after an accident or a stroke disables us. We find a way to deal with the death of someone we love. Sometimes we reset our paths for positive reasons and other times because life has dealt us a blow.

Divorce is one of those blows. Whether you have chosen it or not, your path is being reset.

You do have a choice whether to make the process as happy or unhappy as possible. You may choose to get stuck in your

In a best possible outcome, divorce:

- Allows you to forget and forgive
- Gives you the opportunity to create a positive future for yourself
- Provides both spouses with tools to become better parents and offers a better future for their children.

unhappiness forever, or to make the process as positive as possible. Your choice is: The wiser route or the negative route? Getting stuck or moving forward to your Next Best Life?

MY OWN TURNING POINT

If it weren't for my own life-transforming divorce, I might never have become an attorney.

As the oldest of three girls with supportive and encouraging parents, I had a happy and relatively carefree childhood in the country's heartland, Nebraska. All I wanted to do at 17 was get out of my little town and get away from my parents. So after graduating early from high school, I left town to go to college.

My first night there I met "him"—five years older than me and about ready to graduate. We dated. He graduated. He took a job out of state, even further away from my little home town and my parents. Why not get married and move with him? It would be an adventure (that was about as far as I went in my thinking).

So at the age of 19, I married him. By the time I was 21, we had a daughter. During those years, I became well acquainted with his abusing and boozing. Among these "acquaintances" was having my head repeatedly hit against the windshield of a car, being boot-kicked in the face, and hiding in closets with my daughter

◇◇

Valid Reasons Clients Decide NOT to File for Divorce:

- They realize they're still in love and haven't tried counseling.

- This is the first time they're questioning their marriage.

- Their family wants them to get a divorce.

- A dramatic event has disrupted their otherwise happy marriage–serious illness in the family, the death of a child or parent, the loss of a job.

- Their spouse is a spirit lifter, not a spirit crusher.

so when he came home drunk he wouldn't find us. So there I was, a young mother with no college degree who knew I had to get a divorce for my daughter's and my own survival.

I had to figure out what the heck I was going to do—fast. I needed a job. I needed to pay the rent and take care of my child. I also knew I needed to go back to school.

With student loans, no family in town, and my ex not paying child support, I chose to be a survivor. I lived a threadbare life working multiple jobs, finishing my undergraduate degree and going on to law school. I just wanted not to be financially broke forever, and I wanted my daughter to be proud of me. I certainly never thought I'd be a family law attorney.

As it turned out, my own divorce helped set me on the path to become a very good divorce attorney with great empathy and passion for my clients. Divorce had been a turning point for me, a resetting of my own path that transformed my life in positive ways. Ending my marriage forced me to grow up, not look back, work hard, make a positive plan for my future, and execute it. It helped me choose what I would never tolerate again, and focus on what things I indeed wanted my future to hold. It shaped my goals for charity work, and gave me wisdom to pass onto my daughter. And it makes me happy to say she truly sees me as her role model.

My story tells the big truth that I try to help my clients see: *Divorce is a turning point and you can turn it in a positive direction or not. It's your choice.*

Mediation

One of the most positive ways to resolve your divorce is through mediation. In mediation, both spouses and their attorneys, or the spouses without their attorneys, meet with an independent third party in an effort to resolve outstanding issues and avoid a prolonged court battle. Mediation is one of the sanest ways to dissolve a marriage.

NOT GIVING UP OR GIVING IN

In my decades of practice as a divorce attorney, I've helped hundreds of clients through the divorce process. I represent men, and I represent women. Those with children and without. I settle some cases and go to trial on others. I walk clients through settlements and mediation. I appeal judicial decisions when needed. I create new case law for the future. As a Judge Pro Tem, I've made rulings on cases and mediated settlement conferences. But I've also been cursed at, threatened, and almost assaulted by my clients' spouses. I've had opposing attorneys scream inches from my face, and use draconian and unreasonable war tactics. But I've also worked with opposing attorneys who exhibit refreshingly positive demeanors and professionalism.

And, boy, have I heard it all. From my experience, I can tell you some things I know for sure.

Divorcing for your Next Best Life doesn't mean "sticking it" to your soon-to-be ex (or, as I like to say, your STBX) or walking away with the most toys. When you're using the Wiser Divorce model, it doesn't mean somebody has to win, and somebody has to lose. The "win" is in preserving family, preserving friends, and remembering and appreciating the good in your marriage while also accepting your role in the bad. It means going through the process of divorce with dignity, respect, and grace. It means not giving up or giving in to the negativity, but continuing to pursue the goals that are going to make your life better, happier, and

STBX

We're going to mention the soon-to-be ex throughout the book, so let's get familiar with some shorthand: STBX. Think of it as a hashtag to keep it simple when talking about a soon-to-be-ex.

more complete. It means *separating the emotions of divorce from the business of divorce and envisioning your life as you want it to be when you are free.*

In the Wiser Divorce, everyone wins.

Successful athletes don't just wake up one day to greatness. They train, they plan, they are coached, they wear the right equipment, and they envision their success. Think of preparing for and executing your divorce in the same way by asking yourself these questions:

- What will it take to be successful at this?

- How will I mentally prepare?

- Who will I surround myself with?

- What knowledge do I need to arm myself with?

- What is my positive vision for success after my divorce?

Divorce should be a series of strategic decisions designed to help you rebuild your new life going forward. The first step is to make a decision to divorce strategically, not emotionally, even if your STBX (soon-to-be ex) cannot. This means looking honestly and unflinchingly at yourself, your attitudes, your thoughts, your words, and your behaviors.

This book provides you with the tools and the knowledge you need to tame your emotions, to understand how to work most effectively with the attorney who can help you achieve the best outcome, to understand what "going to court" might really

Divorce at its core:

- Divides assets and debts
- Determines guidelines for parenting children
- Defines future obligations between former spouses.

mean, and to enable you to separate your emotional trauma from the business of resetting your life path.

The goal of this book, like the goal of all my work with divorcing couples, is to translate divorce into a transformative process that won't destroy you emotionally or financially but will lead you positively toward the rest of your life. That's how people achieve the Wiser Divorce.

This book is about making sure your best self shows up during your divorce, which is the first step in claiming your Next Best Life.

2 Get Strategic About Your Divorce

The Wiser Divorce can and does occur.

I'm not making that up. I've participated in many "good" divorces—even a few where people actually shake hands, smile, hold their heads high, and end their marriages in peace.

In the Wiser Divorce, when the ink is dry on the papers, everyone's life is better in ways that really matter. Out of sad and sometimes heartbreaking circumstances, two previously unhappy people can now see their separate futures—futures they can both look forward to. The outcome isn't just about the death of a relationship, but about two people evolving to their best next stage of life.

In the Wiser Divorce, you feel the satisfaction of knowing you did not let your divorce ruin your life or the lives of your children.

MINIMIZING THE HURT

How does this happen? Is it a fluke, as rare as a lightning strike, a chance event that happens for the lucky few who win the divorce lottery?

No. You get a shot at the Wiser Divorce when you, and hopefully, your attorney, decide to pursue positive solutions even if your STBX and the attorney on the other side won't. Even better is when everyone—both spouses *and* their attorneys—make the conscious choice and a determined effort to pursue those positive solutions. That, indeed, is winning the lottery of divorces.

These positive solutions work when we set aside the *emotion* of divorce and focus on the *strategy* of divorce. This doesn't mean there will be no conflict, frustration, or anger at times. But it does mean it will be minimized and dealt with as part of the process, so it is not still with you at the end.

A strategic divorce is one in which two people have made a conscious decision to operate from an emotion-free zone and to deal with the divorce as a series of business decisions.

In an emotional divorce, the focus is on creating blame or pain, or on getting revenge for the life that will be lost. People who engage in divorce as an emotional experience forget that it is, at its core, simply the business of ending a legal relationship. In an emotional divorce, the woman who inherited $40,000 from grandma and used that money to buy a getaway cabin for the family believes that cabin belongs to her, even if she put the cabin in both her and her spouse's name. She believes this even if the law says otherwise. From a legal standpoint in my state, that cabin is joint property that must be divided in some prescribed, equitable way, even if that $40,000 is now worth $100,000 because the cabin's value has increased. From this woman's emotional standpoint, that cabin represents her grandma's legacy and love. Yet she made the choice to give the result of grandma's love to her family, and now it must be divided.

How will this woman's divorce proceed if she stays angry about her choice throughout her divorce instead of accepting the reality of her own actions and moving on? Is staying angry going to be time and energy well spent? Of course not.

Or what about the couple who have excessive credit card debt at divorce because one of them just couldn't stick with their agreed-upon budget? The spouse who stuck with the budget may understandably feel it's wrong to be saddled with a portion of the debt after the divorce. Sorry, but in my state the budget-conscious spouse will likely have to take on a good portion of that debt, as unfair as it may seem. That spouse can whine and cry and kick through the divorce about the unfairness of it all, but the outcome will be the same no matter how hard the more responsible spouse protests. No one gets extra points for being "good" during the marriage.

So the budget-wise spouse can either use up a lot of brain power on negativity about the debt or accept it and move on to

Characteristics of a Strategic Divorce

- Honesty, transparency, and open dialogue
- Early in-person meetings with you, your STBX, and your attorneys
- Respectful communication
- Balanced emotions
- Children come first
- The good that came from the marriage is acknowledged
- The past stays in the past
- Fairness trumps the law
- Both parties embrace a new life
- Everything possible is resolved out of court

something more positive—like setting a time goal for being debt free.

WISING UP: *You can either strategically accept your own actions and move on or color your entire divorce process with anger about choices you may now regret.*

The legal action of divorce is about establishing the terms for concluding the legal relationship you entered into when you married. That may sound harsh, a cold way to end a relationship that started with dreams and promises and love. It's not harsh. It's just realistic. In fact, it's the best way to steer clear of igniting the emotional harshness that marks too many divorces.

A strategic divorce equals a Wiser Divorce. Strategic thinking creates positive solutions.

If you and your STBX can set aside emotions long enough to focus on the strategy that will get you to your Next Best Life, you can win the divorce lottery.

CLEAR VISION FOR THE FUTURE

Positive solutions begin when you decide to pursue a strategic divorce. So what is a strategic divorce?

By definition, a strategic divorce is one in which each party develops a concrete plan for life, post-divorce, with clearly stated goals and priorities that make it possible to let go of the emotional baggage from the marriage. Each party defines the questions they need answered, and learns to understand which of their goals are realistic and which are not. If there are children, each person makes it a priority to ensure happy, successful children who are shielded from conflict.

Being strategic leads to a Wiser Divorce.

Embarking on a strategic divorce is almost like writing a business plan for your Next Best Life (something you'll find in Chapter 10). In fact, **a core characteristic of a strategic divorce is**

Reshaping Your Dream Life

Just thinking about Janet makes me smile.

Janet and her husband were 60. Their children were grown. Janet had spent her entire adult life being the "perfect" wife–dinner on the table every evening, house spotless, children's activities and educational needs met, all while her own dreams were being deferred to concentrate on supporting her husband's career.

And he *had* achieved a stellar professional career.

Then he walked in one evening and announced it was over.

Janet broke down sitting in my office when we first met. In fact, she sobbed through the first four meetings I had with her. She began to find her strength when we started to explore, and I asked her to focus on, what she wanted her life to look like after the divorce was final. To my surprise, she had answers–good answers. She wanted to travel. She wanted to downsize her house.

Oh, and she wanted to be a potter.

She had discovered pottery decades earlier, during a trip to Italy with her sisters, and fell in love with the process of creating art with her own hands. But becoming a potter seemed unrealistic. After all, she wasn't getting any younger. The equipment was expensive. The process was messy. And what practical value did it have for the wife of a successful man to be making pottery?

Now there was nothing to stop her from this impractical and unrealistic dream.

After the divorce Janet studied pottery. She learned to create beautiful art. She recently had her first show. I've seen her pottery and it is amazing.

If she had not been spurred along by the abrupt end of the life she had expected to last forever, Janet would never have opened herself up to fulfilling this dream. When one door closed for Janet, it helped another one open for her. Janet is now more satisfied, happy, and content than she ever thought she could be.

WISING UP: Look at your divorce as a path to doing something you always wanted to do, whatever that may be. Your after-divorce life can look different and be more rewarding than you ever thought possible.

that you come out of it with a clear vision of your future and a real-istic roadmap for bringing that vision to life. In other words, as you go through the process of divorce, you'll know what your life can look like after this marriage is over. It helps take a lot of the fear out of the process. And less fear generally translates into less anger and less need to win at your STBX's expense.

One of your most important first steps, if you want a good outcome for your divorce, is to find the right attorney.

That may sound self-serving, coming from a divorce attorney. But the right attorney understands that a bloody battle to the death will *never* result in a truly successful divorce. Unfortunately, there are still plenty of attorneys today who buy into the old-school model of divorce as war and adversarial, or divorce as litigation designed to name and punish the guilty party. You'll find a thorough discussion on choosing the best attorney for you in Chapter 8.

The right attorney will guide you in the unfamiliar territory of divorce and keep you on track to navigate and create a successful divorce.

With the wrong attorney, you can find yourself on the fast track from marriage hell to divorce hell.

TIMING YOUR NEGOTIATIONS

Engaging in a strategic and wiser divorce also means accepting that nobody will get everything he or she wants, no matter how much collaboration and cooperation and compromise goes on during settlement negotiations. And nobody will get everything they want no matter how hard they fight in front of a judge if they go to trial.

That's why part of your thinking during a strategic divorce has to be about what you can live with. Not what you want, not what you feel you deserve to exact revenge, and not necessarily your desire to maintain the same level of lifestyle. To be sure, there are some things and some decisions you simply cannot nor should not be expected to live with. Not everything has to be negotiable, especially when it comes to your kids. For example, you cannot negotiate equal parenting time with an active drug abuser. It's okay to have some nonnegotiables.

When exploring a strategic divorce settlement, consider two points during the process that offer the optimal chance for a successful negotiated settlement.

One of these optimal moments is near the beginning of the process. Even though there may still be questions to be answered, two spouses at this stage may have a strong sense of what's fair between them. No one is out to stick it to their STBX. No one is being unreasonable. It's possible, at this point, to reach some good negotiated agreements—agreements that will have been reached with minimal fuss and a minimal involvement of attorney time (i.e. money).

A second optimal opportunity is when you have all the information you need and your questions have been answered, but before preparation for the trial has been started (once preparation for trial starts, your attorney bill dramatically increases). With your questions answered, your attorney can tell you what you might expect at trial, which can provide you with a good understanding of what's realistic and what may be considered unreasonable. Once you and your attorney shift into aggressive trial mode, the chances for settlement go down and they can go down fast.

Instead of letting the process of divorce happen to you, take affirmative action. Plan your divorce strategically.

For the sake of preserving your time, your emotional invest-ment, and your financial resources, you will want to take advan-tage of these opportunities and every other opportunity that exists to agree to settlement terms. If you and your STBX aren't enemies yet, it's possible to end on good terms. It's possible to end as co-parents. It's possible to achieve a Wiser Divorce.

COMMUNICATION AND COMPROMISE

One of the most encouraging trends in ending a marriage is the collaborative model for divorce, which is gaining in popularity. This strategic model is focused on transparency, cooperation, and healing rather than the litigious focus of traditional divorce. I am a big proponent of collaborative divorce and see it as a power-fully positive solution in the field of family law. But the strategic aspects of this model can be put in place in any divorce. Think about how you can use these strategies in your own case.

In the collaborative divorce model, each spouse has his or her own attorney who has been trained in the collaborative process. At the beginning, both parties sign an agreement to stick with the collaborative process, which involves a lot of communication

Top 10 Ways to Wise Up About Divorce

1. Hire the right attorney for you.

2. Put your kids first.

3. Prioritize your goals.

4. Understand your settlement options.

5. Understand and accept who your spouse is and isn't.

6. Forgive the bad marriage and your own role in it.

7. Know when to compromise and when to fight.

8. Be honest with your attorney and the judge and with your STBX.

9. Follow your attorney's advice. Follow your attorney's advice. Follow your attorney's advice.

10. Look to the future.

and a lot of compromise. In the state where I practice, there are powerful incentives to stick with the process and find solutions. For example, if you decide to back away from the collaborative model, you are required to hire a different attorney. You cannot use documents that have been prepared by experts who were brought in as part of the collaborative team. In essence, if you decide you are not going to settle but to litigate, you have to start over. Starting over means redoing all the work to that point, and it will definitely add to the cost of your divorce.

In addition to having an attorney, each spouse in the collaborative model has a divorce coach. The coaches help get the underlying emotional and relationship junk off the table and out in the open so the focus can be on the "business" of the divorce.

Communication coaching takes place, helping both spouses learn to wisely communicate and listen to the other. This allows people who may have been living in conflict to begin speaking to each other in a way that facilitates cooperation instead of perpetuating antagonism. Instead of, "I want the boat! You know it ought to be mine—we bought it for me, and you never use it," you might hear, "I'd like you to consider giving me the boat at the lake, since fishing is something I really enjoy doing."

Can you see the difference in how changing the words of a request could affect a response?

After communication coaching, the divorcing partners are led through a process to determine what questions they need answered in order to resolve their divorce, and to establish joint intentions or common goals for their divorce. Examples: *I need to understand the finances of our business. We want to remain co-parents to our daughter. We want to know we can each buy a house when we're done.*

INNATELY FAIR SOLUTIONS

During this collaborative process, all financial information and documentation is fully and openly shared with both clients. A neutral financial expert reviews the data and prepares a report detailing all assets, debts, tax issues, and proposed budgets. Much of the legal advice is shared in front of both spouses. This means pros and cons are discussed transparently. Both sides can hear what might be bad for them and what might be good for them if they decide to litigate. In this style of divorce, what the law says is only one of many options to look at. A collaborative style process allows for creativity and a solution that feels more innately fair to everyone.

Examine *why* you want something. Whatever your list of goals, ask yourself not just *what* you want, but *why* you want it. Be clear with yourself about *how* these goals will change your life in the future. People fight about riding lawn mowers and outdated sofas and rugs the dogs have been shedding on for years. *Really?* Is the rug that important, or is your thinking clouded by emotion?

When children are involved, a child specialist meets with the children and with the parents. After that, the child specialist gives the parents feedback about how to craft a successful plan for co-parenting.

Next, all the issues that must be negotiated are brought to the table. One by one, the issues to be resolved are written on a board and members of the team—spouses, attorneys, and coaches—brainstorm as many outcomes and solutions as possible.

Let's say the first issue is to decide what to do about the house. Solutions that make their way onto the board could be as diverse as giving the house to the children, selling it, or continuing to co-own it. In this kind of session, nothing is off the table.

When the board is full of options, the next question becomes: *Can you live with this option? Okay, how about this option?*

Once all the options have been discussed, and the options both parties can live with are defined, a mutually "favorite" option is chosen for each asset or issue, and a possible divorce scenario is produced in writing by the financial expert. Once everyone has seen that scenario, adjustments are made, and additional written scenarios are created until a scenario is achieved that both spouses can live with.

SAVING MONEY, COURT TIME

This, of course, is what good attorneys will do even if they are not formally engaged in the collaborative process. A good attorney is always asking a client, "What can you live with, and what is worth fighting about?" or "How does this scenario look to you?" Good attorneys explore every possible resolution with their clients, even if it is something a court would not or cannot order. Collaborative-style divorces are some of the most satisfying cases I work on.

Studies show that people who have worked together to craft solutions return to court a lot less often. They may never be buddies, but they've learned how to work together for the common good. And they will save themselves a lot of money if they never again have to set foot in a courtroom.

As a giant step forward in achieving the Wiser Divorce in this country, creative models like this should be explored in every divorce and should happen more often than going to court.

In addition to collaborative divorce, there are many other mediation and settlement options that can lead to success.

Spouses can meet with an independent mediator with or without their attorneys. The job of a professional mediator is to broker a creative settlement with terms everyone can live with. Or the spouses can meet together with just their attorneys to do the same thing. Simply hiring attorneys who are willing to think outside the box of traditional courtroom litigation is the best start. These methods minimize the damage. They help couples achieve a successful, strategic divorce.

PRESCRIPTION FOR AN UNPLEASANT DIVORCE

Maggie and Lew could have had an ugly divorce.[1] While they were both highly intelligent and very nice people, they were opposites in personality. Lew had a more laid-back and easy going personality, which made him sometimes come across as indecisive. Maggie was more of an extrovert and much more direct; there was never a question about where she stood on things. As a result, Maggie had assumed more of a "director" role in their marriage. Yet Lew's hard work in his business had led to their financial well-being.

Take these personality differences, add in the emotions that accompany the end of a marriage, and you have a prescription for a potentially unpleasant divorce.

Lew owned a successful business when he met Maggie. During their marriage the business grew even more successful, and it would be fair to say that he owed some of his success to Maggie's forcefulness. He was very good in his field, but she was also a powerful player behind the scenes. In the same way that she ran the family, she also helped Lew make bolder choices in

---

1   Just a reminder that I've changed names, modified identifying details, and blended stories throughout the book. This protects confidentiality and privacy. All the pertinent details are accurate, and are based on cases actually handled by my firm.

his role as a business owner. That translated into a stronger business than Lew might have been able to build on his own, given his easy-going nature.

Although their personality differences had been complementary and advantageous in business, those differences didn't balance out as well in their role as parents. Maggie and Lew had four children. Their incompatible parenting styles resulting from their personality differences had created conflict during the marriage and threatened to derail negotiations during the divorce.

When fundamental differences come up around the emotionally charged issue of parenting, the tension can spill over into every other issue. Add into the mix a successful and structurally complex business, and the financial terms of the divorce could also become contentious.

In the case of this couple, it was critical to set aside emotions and focus on strategy.

Despite their different personalities, it became clear to both Maggie and Lew that a collaborative model would be better for the children and for their future as co-parents, and would allow them many more options for financial resolution than traditional litigation.

◇◇

Top 10 Lies Divorcing People Tell Themselves

1. This divorce is all my STBX's fault.

2. The divorce process will make my STBX pay for his/her wrongs.

3. "Justice" will be served if I go to court.

4. I won't have to change my life or my attitudes.

5. I should be embarrassed to be divorcing.

6. Everyone in my life must choose sides.

7. The judge will fix everything.

8. My divorce is unique.

9. I won't have to give up anything that matters to me.

10. Somebody, somehow, someday will tell me I'm right.

Through the collaborative process, they learned to communicate better and, in doing so, adopted better ways of interacting and partnering to parent their children. While Lew had not "parented" the children as much as Maggie because of his work obligations, they agreed that an equal time-sharing plan with their children was the best way to ensure their children's emotional well-being.

Their improved communication skills also brought them a better sense of how to cooperate for the best possible outcome in other areas, as well. In negotiating the financial terms of their settlement, Lew agreed to sell some of his business assets so he could provide a generous financial package for Maggie, who was not only the mother of his children but had been a contributor to the success of that business. The up-front settlement amount made possible by Lew's decision to sell business assets would have likely not been forced upon him by a court had Lew and Maggie gone to trial. But the collaborative process lent itself to this creative solution.

Not only that, but because of the coaching that changed the dynamic of this relationship, Lew willingly agreed to provide for Maggie's future, without being resentful or resistant.

Without the coaching, Maggie might have clung to the idea the children should be with her more than Lew because that had been her primary role in the family. These tensions could have colored their future decisions about and interactions with their children, and certainly would have protracted their divorce. The collaborative divorce model changed that dynamic completely.

This divorce had the potential to be ugly and unpleasant, creating a permanent fracture that would have impacted their children for years to come.

Instead, Maggie and Lew achieved a healthy divorce, and have both moved on to independent happy and healthy lives, while still co-parenting their children. While Maggie and Lew agreed to a collaborative style divorce, this kind of divorce can be achieved in any divorce model.

WISING UP: *Accept the differences that are ending your marriage, communicate, be creative and honor your spouse's contribution to the marriage and your children.*

PEACE OF MIND

In the Wiser Divorce, both people can move on with their self-respect intact. You and your STBX have both acted in a way that preserves your respect for each other. Each person acknowledges who the other person is, and where that person is coming from, even if they don't agree. You will be better able to walk away without intense hatred for your STBX. You'll feel that you had your questions answered, which gets you to the peace of mind you deserve. And you will understand your obligations under the divorce.

In the Wiser Divorce, you will have planned for the best and most fair financial outcome for both parties, even if that means your finances look different after divorce than if you had stayed together (this inevitably happens and you need to accept it). You will understand the reasons for the outcome. You will have a financial plan and a budget in place for your own future, as well as clarity about whether you'll be re-educating, going back to work, moving, or making other major adjustments.

Equally important, the Wiser Divorce—a strategic divorce—will allow you to view the divorce not as the definition of your life but as just a transition in your life.

Most important of all, if you have children, you will be better able to co-parent. You will have a plan for continuing to work together as parents, and you will understand how to relate to each other in a way that is healthy and healing for your children and for yourself. By your actions you will have minimized the impact of divorce on your children.

In an ideal world, you would never see a courtroom as part of your divorce proceedings. As more divorcing people become aware of this different way of approaching divorce and seek out attorneys who are willing to help them divorce strategically instead of emotionally or combatively, we will increase the number of Wiser Divorces. Even if you are already in a divorce that is headed down the wrong path, you can change it now simply by changing your own thoughts, words and actions. The face of the

Follow Your Attorney's Advice

Here's what it can look like when you don't follow your attorney's advice, and you deny the truth of your future.

I kept telling Rachel to hire someone to help her create a post-divorce financial plan. She was expecting a $600,000 settlement and, not having been the one who handled the finances in her financially comfortable family, that sounded like a lot of money to Rachel. But I could see she was getting ready to make some serious mistakes.

Rachel had been blinded by all those zeroes in her settlement agreement.

As soon as she had her settlement, despite not having a job or being qualified for a good one without retraining, Rachel paid $400,000 cash for a house and $80,000 for a car. With no job and not having worked in years, Rachel had the unrealistic expectation of hanging onto her previous lifestyle with only $120,000 in cash left from her settlement.

Two years later, the real estate market tanked.

Rachel now owned a house that was worth far less than she had paid for it. She had spent almost all of the $120,000, her car was worth much less than its purchase price and she found herself forced to sell her house. She only received $200,000 after the sale. That's all she had left for the rest of her life.

WISING UP: Trying to hang onto or trying to recreate your old life is not strategic and is likely to be very costly. When you're planning your Next Best Life, make a financial plan. And if your attorney is saying your financial plan isn't realistic, pay attention.

divorced family can be changed, one family at a time. One person at a time, society can move to a place where divorce begins to lose some of its negative baggage.

The first step is to stop the flow of negative energy into your divorce and begin to pour positive energy into the divorce process.

When a business partnership ends, we don't attach the stigma we do to divorce. It's a legal relationship. It's transitioning to its next life stage. It's not a failure. We can begin to think of divorce in the same way—as a transition. A legal relationship is ending, but not your life. In fact, your best new life is just beginning!

3

Resist the Lure of Negative Emotions

I want to tell you another one of my most positive divorce stories.

Anna and her husband, Robert, had been married almost 20 years. She and her husband started out as certified public accountants and business partners. Both were very linear, black-and-white thinkers.

In their mid-forties, they were successful professionals with three children, none of whom were yet out of high school. They respected and loved each other. So far, so good.

Then Anna had an epiphany: She was not living the life she was called to live. She realized that she had been ignoring her strong intuitive nature for years in favor of all that linear, black-and-white thinking. She started to pay attention to an inner voice that revealed things to her that she shouldn't logically know. Her spiritual nature began to flourish. She came to understand that her intuition, once unleashed, was more than intuition. People around the country began to hire her for her psychic abilities.

For Anna, this felt like her life calling.

For Robert, it felt like a betrayal of the life they had built over two decades.

People change during marriage. What might have been the perfect fit when both people are 23 might not work at all after two decades. People develop different wants, different expectations, different interests and goals in life. Are you going to be angry because your partner changed over 10, 20, or 30 years? People who are happily married by the time they reach their silver wedding anniversary may have worked at it; however, there's at least a little bit of luck involved, too, that they didn't just grow in completely different directions.

Knowing it would mean a huge financial hit, Anna decided to walk away from accounting and embrace her new life as a spiritualist and a psychic. She began to travel, visiting and interviewing healers around the world.

Divorce seemed inevitable. But Anna was committed to ending her marriage with as little pain and disruption as possible. That's when she came to me. We discussed how to walk through the legal process in ways that were not soul-killing.

Robert, after some initial skepticism, saw that the marriage could end without destroying their family—or their relationship.

During the course of negotiating positive solutions for a Wiser Divorce, Anna and Robert felt so good about each other and their relationship that they briefly considered trying to stay together. They were one of the most caring and evolved couples I've ever encountered. Ultimately, they accepted the reality that they were no longer the two people who started out together two decades earlier. Anna no longer fit within the life that still worked for Robert. Robert's life no longer worked for Anna. They were no longer good partners for each other.

That didn't stop them from negotiating a new way of being in an ongoing relationship as parents to their three children. They ended up buying a second house five doors away from the house they had owned together, so their children could go back and forth with minimal disruption.

Robert and Anna proved to be grown-up enough to acknowledge their sadness without blaming each other. That enabled them to complete the legal process of divorce with a minimum of pain. And because I am still in touch with Anna, I know that Robert, Anna and their children remain a happy and successful family, even though their family looks different than they thought it would.

WISING UP: Just because you and your STBX are at different places in your life than when you married doesn't mean either of you are bad. It just means you evolved in different ways. Accept that reality, protect your children, and move forward without blame. *You don't have to be overwhelmed by your emotions.*

HEALING THE WOUNDS

Anna and Robert's example proved to me that divorce can be far more than just civilized, which is sometimes the most positive outcome people can imagine. Anna and Robert proved to me that a Wiser Divorce can result in a positive transformation for the entire family.

To make that happen, most people need to make a significant shift away from their first impulse when divorce becomes inevitable—which is to react emotionally. And, of course, most of those initial emotions will be negative. Fear. Pain. Shock. Anger.

You can try really hard and sometimes a marriage just doesn't work out. But you don't have to launch a war to end it.

The first and most critical step in creating a divorce that results in a positive transformation is a commitment to eliminate the negativity from the process and replace it with a positive outlook. Negative thinking is a poison. Like any poison, it's systemic. It multiplies like a virus, spreading everywhere, destroying everything it touches.

The evolved divorce moves quickly from our hearts to our heads. The change starts with the way we *think* about divorce, which leads to changes in the way we *speak* and *act* during our divorce.

This way of approaching divorce essentially allows us to heal the wounds from our marriage. And it starts with the choice of refusing to be at the mercy of our emotions.

LIES WE TELL OURSELVES

What are the thoughts that contribute to the poison of negative thinking? The first is that divorce is the source of your unhappiness. The second is that finding someone to blame will somehow mitigate the pain of divorce. The third is that divorce ruins your entire life. All three thoughts are wrong. They're lies people tell themselves out of pain, fear, and anger.

First lie: *Divorce is the source of your unhappiness.* **The truth:** *The Wiser Divorce gets you out of the unhappiness.*

Divorce does not descend like some kind of black magic

on happy marriages. Divorce happens in unhappy marriages. I promise you, even if divorce came into your life as a bombshell dropped by your STBX, an honest look at your circumstances will reveal the cracks in the relationship. Look hard and look without the rose-colored glasses. You'll see where the communication has diminished, where the emotional intimacy has broken down, where sex has become strained or infrequent or even a distant memory.

Divorce doesn't enter the picture when the marriage is healthy.

So why focus on divorce as the source of your unhappiness? Instead, acknowledge divorce as the first step in regaining your happiness.

One of the most cowardly things people do is stay in an unhappy marriage and refuse to make a move until they find somebody else to take the place of a spouse. An affair is a lousy substitute for courage.

Second lie: *Blaming the other person eases the hurt.* **The truth:** *When blame is the focus, the hurt lingers.*

One of the first impulses when divorce enters the picture is to attach blame. That may start innocently enough with the desire to look for a cause, to understand why the marriage is breaking apart. Thanks to the adversarial nature of divorce law, looking for a cause can quickly derail into the train wreck of blame. Remember, filing for divorce is essentially filing a lawsuit, and lawsuits are intended to determine who's wrong, and who's the victim. Proceeding with that mindset is the antithesis of a Wiser Divorce.

Instead of accepting that sometimes divorce may be the best next stage of a relationship that has run its course, or one that wasn't right to begin with, so many of us feel we need to validate our decision to divorce by pointing a finger at the other person. *There! He's the bad one! Not me! She's at fault! I'm not to blame!*

Unfortunately, focusing on blame also keeps you focused on the problem instead of the solution. And all the pain is found in the problem; healing and moving on are found in the solution. Focusing on blame places your need to have answers or be the "good guy" over your desire to have as much peace of mind as possible during a period of disruption and distress.

Even when there is a bad act or a betrayal of some kind, it's a lot more helpful to get past the bad act to the real root of the problem. Quite honestly, if your STBX was having an affair or engaged in some other bad act, ask yourself: Is this really the person I even want to be with?

When you look honestly at what was happening in the marriage, when you reflect upon your own unmet needs, you will likely see that moving on is best for both of you.

◇◇◇

Rewriting History

Divorce often gets ugly because people get caught up in the emotional battle to rewrite the history of their marriages. Most often this comes down to wanting to erase something that has been done to them—betrayals or lies or abandonment.

The process of divorce can't erase the things others have done. What you can do is shift into an emotion-free zone and remember that things may have been done but they do not define who you are, how you should act, or how you will be. You can refuse to be a victim.

One step in refusing to be a victim is to accept the truth about the marriage—the good, the bad and the ugly. That includes owning the parts you played.

So many people I encounter who cling to a dead marriage have normalized the dysfunction in their homes. They forget about the hugs they aren't getting, the love that isn't happening, the lack of communication, the betrayals.

Once people get past the idea that they have a marriage worth salvaging, they are often surprised to realize how much they've been missing in life.

So would you rather be right, or would you rather be happy? Even if you are right, does it help your divorce to keep asserting that fact? Remember, there is no gold medal at the end of a divorce for the "good guy," even if you think you deserve one.

The sooner we realize we can be happy without insisting on being in the right, or having someone validate that we are right, the faster we get to happy.

Third lie: *Divorce means your life is ruined.* **The truth:** *Divorce does not define the rest of your life.*

Divorce does not have to be the movie reel that repeats over and over again. Yet we tend to keep running those old reels over and over in our heads: *He did this. She did that. Here's what he said. Here's how she treated me.* You can choose to keep replaying those old movies. Or you can change the reel. You can shoot new movies. Nothing stays the same forever.

Unless you choose to let it.

DRINKING THE POISON

I asked one of my clients to make a list of all the good things about her children's relationship with their father. She said there weren't any.

I didn't believe her. If everything related to this man, who fathered her children, whom she **chose** to father her children, was so bad, she wouldn't be so angry and bitter that he filed for divorce. She'd be ecstatic to be rid of him. She would have filed herself, long before he got around to it. Instead, she's wasting physical and emotional and mental energy on bitterness, on calling him names, on finding new ways to express how much she loathes him—and tragically wanting and expecting her children to do the same.

When you divorce from the place of your negative emotions, the ramifications don't end when divorce is completed. The fall-out can continue. Some people who let negative emotions dominate carry those wounds their whole lives.

What if she could find a way to take the same amount of energy and focus it on naming the good that came out of their marriage and finding a way to carry that good forward, into their next stage of life as a divorced family?

It takes so much more energy not to get along than it takes to get along. It takes more brain power and muscles and face twitches. It's mentally exhausting. There's no energy left over for walking through the day with a smile.

Yes, you can smile through a divorce.

Sometimes we behave as if our anger and our revenge and our bitterness will somehow be payback for our STBX. If we walk through our divorces with that point of view, the joke is on us: Our misery isn't making our STBX unhappy. It's making *us* unhappy! We're feeding our own misery! We're sinking deeper into an emotional slump. We're drinking the poison but hoping it will kill someone else. We're using energy we could use to dream new dreams or shower more love on our children or learn strategies that will heal us more quickly and more thoroughly. We're squandering our emotional energy to make ourselves unhappier.

Cut that out! It's *your* choice whether or not you smile through your divorce.

Even if you're only faking it at first, making that choice begins to turn it into reality. What you do becomes your reality.

Prove it to yourself. The next time you're in a bad mood at the grocery store, make a conscious decision to smile your best smile for the cashier. If she has a nametag, call her by name. Look her in the eyes when you smile at her. Wish her a terrific day. I promise, by the time you walk away with your bag of groceries, you'll feel better than you felt when you got in line with a frown on your face and a sour thought in your head. Your behavior impacts your brain.

The more you *act* it, the more you *are* it.

When we apply that principle to divorce, we sometimes find that the best revenge is to allow our STBX to see how entirely unmiserable we are.

◇◇

STBXs Behaving Badly

Sometimes the emotional behavior of a STBX is so bad it's laughable. Sometimes it makes you want to cry. Do you want to be these people? I hope not. Here are a few standouts from my years as a divorce attorney:

- **Irretrievable memories:** Buddy was on his second marriage–and his second divorce. His son from his first marriage died from cancer when he was barely a teenager. As the second marriage began to falter, Buddy moved out of the house, leaving behind some of his personal belongings while negotiations were still up in the air. His STBX grew irate, then vindictive. In scavenging through the attic, she turned up the only box of belongings and memories–including birthday and Christmas cards his deceased son had written–that Buddy still had to remind him of his son. The STBX burned these memories.

  WISING UP: Remember the adage from your mother that you shouldn't do anything you don't want the public to read about on the front page of the paper? Remember that in your divorce. Hateful acts not only make you look like a jerk, they also perpetuate your own unhappiness.

- **STBX meltdown:** Mac was a direct descendent of Thomas Jefferson, signer of the Declaration of Independence. Mac had a number of original letters authored by Jefferson that had been handed down through his family. His STBX sold the letters on eBay at a fraction of their value. Dumb move, dear. You may now owe him money for selling his personal family heirlooms.

WISING UP: Think before you play the revenge game. Dumb moves during your divorce can cost you dearly in the end.

- **Girl's best friend:** Chloe and Will had some very good years, financially. At one point when there was plenty of extra cash, the couple decided to get the top items on their individual wish lists. He bought the vintage car of his dreams; she got a very flashy diamond ring, equal in value to the car. When Will added regular drug use to his wish list, Chloe came to me to handle the divorce. They agreed early on that he would keep the car, and she would keep the ring. Just before Will's deposition, Chloe mentioned that her diamond had a big chip in it. I think we all know that real diamonds don't easily chip. Backed into a corner, Will admitted in his deposition that the ring he had presented to Chloe to balance his vintage car extravagance was not a diamond—it was cubic zirconium. In the end Chloe drove away with the vintage car **and** the fake diamond.

WISING UP: Somehow, some way, the truth usually comes out during a divorce. Own it up front.

- **Breaking up:** Ursula married late in life. One of her most treasured possessions was her collection of Dresden figurines. Worth many thousands of dollars, the figurines represented a lifelong passion for Ursula. During the divorce, we had to obtain a court order for Ursula's STBX to bring the Dresden collection to my office, so we could assess their value for purposes of the settlement agreement. In a classic example of cutting off his nose to spite his face, this STBX instead dumped hundreds of the figurines in the lobby of my office. Many of them broke. His petty act made a not-so-petty difference when it was decided how much money Ursula would receive because of the monetary value of the property he destroyed, and also because it cast him in such a bad light in the eyes of the judge making the determination.

WISING UP: Bad acts not only can cost you money, but they can impact the outcome if you have to go to court.

An added benefit: Coming into the proceedings with a smile on our faces almost always helps us achieve more of what we hope to achieve in negotiations. It can completely turn around a situation in which people typically bring their worst selves to the table and not their best selves.

CHOOSE YOUR MENTAL STATE

Choosing to focus on the positive instead of giving into negative emotions does not mean you need to sweep your hurt or your anger or your grief under the rug. Strategic divorce isn't about denying the pain you're going through.

Your strategic and emotionally healthy divorce simply allows you to choose which mental state you want to bring to the legal process of your divorce. It is essentially a decision to either focus on achieving a positive outcome during the legal proceedings, or to allow your emotions to rule while you negotiate the business and legal terms of redefining your relationship with your STBX.

Divorce is a legal process. Divorce is a series of business decisions. Divorce is a strategic negotiation.

◇◇◇

Words, Thoughts and Actions

Wouldn't we all rather end up with a good divorce instead of spending time, money, and emotional energy wading through Divorce Hell? A good divorce starts by creating that emotion-free zone where you can focus on the thoughts, words and actions that break old relationship patterns. This creates an environment for strategic decision-making.

- **Thoughts:** processing your divorce with understanding, not blame;

- **Words:** committing to healthy communication;

- **Actions:** putting compromise, relationships and fairness first.

The best legal, business, and strategic decisions get made in an emotion-free zone.

I often suggest to my clients that they can create an emotion-free zone by thinking of their divorce as a series of rooms. We're going to put the divorce negotiations in one room, and when we are in that room, we are going to focus on strategic decisions about life goals and priorities and finances. There may be a room for handling their children as part of the divorce—the place where they talk about the children together, a place where they talk to the children together, a place where the children come first and all discussions about co-parenting take place. They have a room for interacting with friends and family during the divorce. And they have another room for all the pain and grief and rage associated with the end of their marriage. All those emotions are valid and deserve to be dealt with. I encourage them to get all the help they need when the time is right to enter those rooms.

It doesn't help you to knock down the walls between those rooms. The walls serve a good purpose. The walls allow you to bring healing and health to every part of your life. The walls give you space to transform your life in the best possible way.

BEATING THE BULLDOG

Am I a Pollyanna, unrealistically expecting something positive during one of life's toughest blows? It's OK if you think so. But I have personally seen the difference that people's attitudes, words, and behaviors have on their divorce process and their lives after divorce. The difference is startling.

Some divorce attorneys have a reputation for being a bulldog. People seek them out because they're known for whipping up on STBXs and their attorneys. Some people seek out the bulldog attorneys solely because they don't want to end up facing them across a negotiation table.

I can certainly be a bulldog if forced to do so.

When it comes to my perspective on divorce, I'll gladly take the label Dr. Happy, as one of my clients calls me.

At the end of the day, my clients who set aside their emotions to focus on healthy and positive solutions end up with better results than the most vicious bulldog can achieve. They transform their lives in all the ways that matter most.

Shouldn't that be how we measure how well divorce works?

4   Survive the Initial Shock

Even if you're the one initiating the divorce, ending a marriage brings up a lot of emotions. Many of those emotions may be negative.

You may feel some relief. You may feel some excitement, even, if the marriage has been especially tough, and you can already envision the fresh start you want to make. Mixed with any positive emotions you have, you may also feel fear, guilt, vindictiveness, loss, hatred, hopelessness, depression, bitterness, loneliness, desperation, anger—the list of negatives seems limitless.

And if you're on the receiving end of someone else's decision to divorce, you may also experience shock, which can be paralyzing at a time when you need to be at the top of your game for decision-making.

Before you can make the best choices about how to move forward into the divorce process, you need to do some of the emotional processing necessary to get to the healthy zone we talked about in the previous chapter. I'm not talking about a full emotional recovery; that may take more time than you have before the legal process is set in motion and begins to rearrange your life, requiring that you make some decisions. However, some degree of emotional adjustment has to begin before you can participate in a healthy way to think about launching your Next Best Life. Without some emotional adjustment, you'll be making decisions out of fear, loss and anger, even in a state of shock.

That's not the pathway to a Wiser Divorce. It won't give you the foundation for positive solutions. That's not how divorce works to achieve the best outcome for your family.

◇◇

The Tech Genius & the Musician

Lori and Terry had been married ten years. They had children, twins who were grade-schoolers.

When they met, Terry had a career in technology, but Lori's career superseded his: Lori is a successful musician. And the wants and needs of musicians sometimes overshadow the lives of everyone around them. Even families become part of the entourage that makes it possible for successful musicians to be superstars. So when the babies came along two years into the marriage, Terry decided to be a stay-at-home dad.

Despite the fact that Lori's career came first, Terry had decided that since the twins were in school, he would launch another tech start-up. In his logical approach to life, this made perfect sense, although Lori realized—and resented the fact—that it would mean he would no longer be living at the whim of her somewhat erratic career or continuing the role of a stay-at-home dad.

About this time, it also became clear to Terry that Lori was not going to stop engaging in her rock-star lifestyle, which included flings with groupies. Terry's logical thinking kicked in. He was ready to deal with the facts.

Fact: Lori was a musician, and having one-night stands on the road had become part of her lifestyle.

Fact: The marriage had never been that good.

Fact: The marriage had created an eight-year gap in his career.

Fact: Taking the time to launch a start-up could help him overcome this professional gap and get on with his life.

Fact: Lori was a good mother, and their children loved and needed her.

Fact: There was going to be a positive outcome.

Terry amazed me with his ability to be so matter-of-fact about his future and the future of his children. His only real concern was a fear planted in him by his buddies who had experienced divorce: She's going to try to take your children, and the courts always side with the mother.

I assured Terry that the system would give very little weight, if any, to his STBX's status as mother, or to any assertions that his role in a start-up meant he wouldn't have time to be a fit custodial parent. She would not be able to take the children away, no matter how rich or famous she might be. Being the "mother" no longer carries the automatic advantage it once did.

Terry's logical mindset allowed him to add that fact to the rest of the facts he was operating from. It set his mind at ease and made it possible for him to navigate the settlement discussions from a place of calm instead of from a place of fear.

When we had our first meeting with Terry's STBX and her attorney, we came up with a plan for the twins to continue their relationship with their mother, even when she was on the road touring, that met everyone's needs. It was a creative solution that worked beautifully under their unique circumstances. When Lori is out of town during her time with the children, and they aren't in school, Terry's self-employed status allows him to fly in with the children. The children stay overnight with Lori and a nanny. Terry stays at a nearby hotel and can be with the children when Lori is on stage.

It's a creative and cooperative plan that's not disruptive to the children. No threats and no problems with parenting time.

WISING UP: Try to process your divorce from a place of logic. List the good and the bad, envision a positive outcome, and honor your spouse's relationship with your children, even if he or she wasn't a good spouse to you.

I wish I had before-and-after photos of all my clients. People come in to start the divorce process looking beaten down, all the light gone from their eyes, the sadness just pulling their faces down. When the divorce is over, most of them look years younger. The light is back in their eyes. As hard as divorce is, staying in a soul-killing marriage is much harder.

REFRAMING YOUR LIFE

What you want to move toward in the early stages of processing the fact you are going to be divorced is a place of acceptance.

- You need to *accept the loss of the forever life* you thought, at least at some point, you were living.

- You need to *accept your STBX for who and where he or she is*, no matter what role that played in getting the marriage to this point.

- You need to *accept whatever responsibility you have* for the divorce or for staying in an unhappy marriage—a marriage rarely ends solely because of one person's actions.

- You need to *accept reality*. This is happening. You are going to be divorced. That's harsh, but it is a reality.

One of the most difficult things for some people to give up is what they thought their life together was going to look like. When people marry, they see themselves in love forever, retiring together, maybe playing with grandchildren together or enjoying hobbies or traveling together. Then one day they wake up to the initial shock of realizing that the dream is over. Your role as the dad who comes home every night to help put his kids to bed is over. Your role as the homemaker and hostess for your successful husband is over. Your role as lover and best friend and life partner is over. Your role as the perfect spouse with the perfect home in the perfect suburb is over. Even your identity within your circle of family and friends may be over.

The old dream is dead. And that can be heartbreaking, even when we tell ourselves that our Next Best Life is ahead.

Divorce can be particularly unsettling for spouses when their marital roles have been very separate and defined. One spouse may have been the breadwinner spending many hours away from home to procure financial stability for the family, and the other may have been the primary caregiver and keeper of the home and the children. For those who have been stay-at-home spouses, this business of reframing their lives can feel particularly disruptive. Their home has been their domain, and they don't want to let it go.

If your spouse has been the at-home spouse, and you've been the worker, think how you would feel if you were suddenly forced to give up your job or professional identity just because of your divorce. Stay-at-home spouses many times come to me floundering, terrified. Keeping their home, their primary identity, is a solution if they have a lot of money. In some cases, they may not have been called upon to earn the money to provide for themselves for decades. Suddenly, they're faced with remaking every aspect of their lives and stepping into a role for which they may feel completely unprepared. That's an enormous adjustment. Their entire identity is being ripped away.

So if you have been the earner, try to imagine having your entire day-to-day existence threatened.

Those who have been the primary financial providers may feel the financial successes they achieved belong to them and them alone. They may feel they are entitled to the fruits of their labor, which exist only because of the life hours they alone spent hard at work, and that their spouse has all the smarts and ability needed to make it on their own financially. They may feel their financial estate would be larger if their spouses had not spent as extravagantly or frittered away their earnings. Or maybe they always wanted their spouses to return to work or to enhance their earning prospects, and their spouses refused.

So if your spouse is the earner, try to understand how he or she may feel about spending so many hours away from home to provide for your family, and the hard work and stress your spouse has shouldered alone in order pay the bills and create the family's lifestyle.

Both perspectives must start with accepting the fact that today's reality is over. You cannot rewrite the history of the marriage you chose to live.

After divorce, the roles you established in marriage will inevitably change. The breadwinner may cut back on work hours in order to see the children more because the children won't be there at the end of every work day or work week. The breadwinner may have to support the STBX in a way that feels unfair.

On the other hand, the day-in, day-out caretaker of the children and home may have to find ways to earn income on their own. Full-time parents and homemakers may have to adjust to sharing the responsibilities for the children, an arena which may have felt like their own personal domain.

Accepting these changing realities may not happen overnight. But you need to start the process of accepting the roles established and decisions made during the marriage, and the changes in these roles that may come in the future.

ACCEPT THE IMPERFECTION

The next thing to accept is your STBX.

She's not perfect. He screwed up big time. She did things that feel like they'll hurt forever. He placed his business before your family. She let her family criticize you and belittle you and come between you. He spent money you don't have. She never took enough responsibility for disciplining the children or sticking to a budget or running the household efficiently.

How long are you going to lug that baggage around and use it as an excuse to be miserable?

Your STBX isn't perfect, but neither are you. No marriage is perfect. But most of us do the best we can at a given time. We do what we know how to do. Accept the imperfection. Accept the fact that everyone's best efforts weren't quite enough to make the marriage work. That's how you move on and into your Next Best Life.

While you're accepting your STBX's imperfection, accept your own. Take an appropriate degree of responsibility for where the marriage is today. Maybe you played a significant role in the marriage ending—you shut down emotionally or had an affair or poured all your emotional energy into the children or a job or an addiction. Maybe you think you're the picture of dinner-on-the-table soccer mom or bringing-home-the-bacon dad who had no idea anything was wrong until your spouse dropped the bomb one night when the kids were out with the neighbor kids.

It may be time to accept the fact that you were in denial. Something was wrong.

What were you doing that enabled you to remain oblivious until it was too late to salvage the relationship? What choices did you make that allowed you to remain stuck in a marriage that wasn't working? Accepting responsibility and your new reality will be more productive than getting mad about all the time you "wasted."

EMBRACING HOPE

The dream may be over, but your life isn't, even if that's how it feels in your worst moments. The path is different, and what makes it scary is that people can't see where it's going to lead them.

You can either embrace your divorce as a journey to your Next Best Life, or you can hang on with both hands to that illusion of a dream life. And it *is* an illusion. If that dream were reality, you would not be in the middle of a divorce.

More times than I can count, I've seen sad or angry or defeated people transformed over the course of a year into happy, contented people with new dreams and a new vision of the future. At the end of the divorce process, people who embrace the hope of a new life never look like the same people who walked into my office. People inevitably look more free, more at peace, sometimes even years younger.

Resisting the reality of the marriage and its end is one of the top reasons people turn divorce into an ugly battle. They want to blame the person who announced the decision to divorce, instead of accepting responsibility for the fact they stayed, or the fact that they participated in decisions that are now making the divorce more painful.

A judge is not going to undo decisions you and your spouse made and lived with for years. From a judge's perspective, you could have left your spouse a long time ago if his or her unwillingness to work outside the home was an issue. From a judge's perspective, the fact that one spouse continued to stay in the marriage while another drained the family's savings in order to feed an addiction does not mean the non-addicted spouse gets everything. Staying was the non-addicted spouse's decision.

Once the marriage is ending, it's too late to demand that the divorce process somehow reverse what you chose to live with.

Accept reality. The marriage is over. Fighting the fact won't change a thing. Except possibly make it worse.

SAD, MAD AND I DON'T CARE

Everybody has heard about the stages of grief. Facing divorce is its own kind of grief, of course, and processing the stages of divorce can impact when and how your divorce gets resolved. The stages of processing a divorce that I see most often in my clients are: Sad, Mad and I (gleefully) Don't Care (and I'm ready for my new life!)

Sad is experienced most acutely by the person who did not plan for a divorce. In the Sad Stage, people need gentleness. They don't need to be pushed. They usually need reassurance and an attorney who will take time with them, focus on the first simple steps that must be taken, and help them understand the legal process that's being launched. A good attorney won't push, but will take things gently during this stage. This applies not only to the Sad person's attorney, but to the other attorney as well.

It also applies to the spouse who initiated the move toward divorce; that STBX needs to be patient while the other STBX adjusts to the shock.

Attempting to force someone in the Sad Stage to make drastic changes or major decisions at this time can backfire. I've seen STBXs attempt to get things moving by cutting off the credit cards or checking account, or saying they have to get rid of the car. It's like kicking someone when they're down. And it's going to cost you good will—and probably money—later in the process. It will be expensive, either emotionally or financially.

Sometimes both people have gone through the Sad Stage before they file. People don't jump over this stage, but they may have dealt with the Sad Stage silently during the marriage.

I can help you with Sad. I can wait with you. As an attorney, I can't do much with Mad.

ACTING OUT OF ANGER

The Mad Stage is when people start flinging insults.

She never carried her weight in this family anyway.

The other woman can have him; she'll find out what it's like when he spends more on his car than he spends on the family.

Many people have legitimate reasons to be angry. Their STBX lied, cheated, squandered money, stomped on their dreams, even abused them or their children.

Sometimes Mad allows people to justify doing things that shouldn't be done. Sometimes it seems to give them permission to assert their newfound independence in unreasonable ways because they've now realized they allowed themselves to be controlled or silenced during their marriage. *It's their fault, and I'm not going to take responsibility for being part of a failed marriage.* These are often people who didn't deal with problems during the marriage and now want to. Or it's their way of asserting that they didn't do anything bad. Mad can be a stand-in for Not My Fault.

Even if you are angry, you still have to look at the process of divorce as a series of business decisions. You can be mad, and you likely will be at some point, but being mad is not the same as acting out and making decisions from your anger.

Wallowing too long or getting stuck in the Mad Stage is never, ever going to have a good outcome. Bad behavior during the Mad Stage can easily come back to bite you when you end up in front of a judge who may make decisions about your life based on what he knows about your most immature, anger-fueled choices. That's what Mad gets you.

If you can't get over it yet, do your best to hide your Mad. But you can and should get over it at some point, because staying mad for the long term will slowly poison you and those you love.

Remember that imaginary house where you can compartmentalize all the different ways of reacting to your divorce? At some point, you have to leave Mad and Sad in your counseling room and come with me into the attorney room.

Divorce may be a time when you make the most significant financial decisions you will make in your entire life. Divorce can also have the most profound positive or negative effect on children as anything your children will ever experience. As an attorney, I can help you look strategically at different options and the impact on assets, taxes, and budget. I can help you help your children. But you have to engage with me on this. I know you are mad or sad, but let's sit in this room—in the attorney room—and make some strategic decisions.

Giving More Than You're Required to Give

Hannah and Gerald were well into their careers when they married, both for the second time. During almost two decades of marriage, her career continued to climb and his business declined. By the time they decided to divorce, he had been diagnosed with multiple sclerosis and could no longer work.

The house they lived in had been inherited by Hannah, and in our state therefore would be hers in a divorce. It was a house she had furnished as her dream house. But the house was also ideally set up for Gerald as his health and mobility continued to decline.

Having made up her mind to bring her best self to the divorce, Hannah agreed to settlement terms that would enable Gerald to buy her dream house for less than fair market value. She said to me, "What's most important for me is to end this gracefully and not be bitter. In the end, leaving this marriage on good terms is more important than money."

WISING UP: Bring your best self to your divorce, and remember that some things are more important than money.

◇◇

The Brain's Emotional Highway

Science has shown there is a significant difference in the way men and women process emotional information. Biology has built a super-highway between a woman's left and right brain. For good or bad, Mother Nature didn't do that for most men.

What does this mean? Even in emotionally charged situations, women typically can zip around more easily between both sides of their brain, giving them a greater ability to quickly connect emotion with logical thought. I see this in mediation, where women can more swiftly connect the decisions that make sense logically and the options that resonate emotionally. Because they can connect logic and emotion faster–and note the difference–they tend to be able to make decisions quicker in emotion-packed settings. This also means women tend to relate facts with emotion and may need more guidance in focusing on just the facts. They also may look for ways to compromise even at their own expense.

Men, generally speaking, sometimes have to go much more slowly. While they can more easily relate facts without emotion, they need longer to process options and reach decisions when the topic is emotionally charged because mechanically the male brain doesn't switch tracks as quickly. Studies have shown[1] men take up to seven hours longer, on average, than women for their brain to process emotional input.

This is not a slam on men or women. It is what scientific research tells us. And everyone should be cognizant of this possible difference in processing divorce options. If you need time to process your options, take the time and don't let anyone hurry you. Men may need time alone to think about settlement options. Women may need to be forced to take time, so they don't regret their decisions later. This is probably why successful divorce negotiations may take hours and hours before a result is reached that everyone can live with. If you process faster than your STBX, don't become frustrated. Let him–or her–have the time needed to make decisions he–or she–can live with and feel he–or she–participated in.

---

1   Anne Moir and Bill Moir, Why Men Don't Iron: The Fascinating and Unalterable Differences Between Men & Women (New York: Citadel, 1999).

EMOTIONAL REVENGE VS. STRATEGIC NEGOTIATION

Eric was reeling when he came to me. The father of four children, he had caught his wife having sex with their female nanny, a college student who was only a few years older than their oldest son.

This discovery felt like a violation on multiple levels, and left Eric reeling with shock.

He filed for divorce right away. The enormity of the betrayal propelled him to quick action. But he was far from being ready, mentally and emotionally, to finalize things. He was still in shock. We can all imagine how shocking it is to walk in on a spouse actually in the act of cheating. This revelation, for Eric, went way beyond the shock of merely finding his wife in a motel with a stranger. It also seemed like a betrayal of their children, who looked up to their nanny as a caregiver, an authority figure—even, in some ways, like a big sister.

Eric's wife, of course, was out of the marriage already.

I helped Eric slow down enough to make smart decisions instead of vindictive decisions, as much for the sake of his children as anything. He wanted to reveal what was going on to all their friends and neighbors—an action that would have embarrassed his children, his wife, and himself.

Ultimately, Eric kept his house and primary care of his children. But I helped him see that publically proclaiming the truth about his STBX's behavior would be far too damaging to their children. The affair was not illegal in any way, although the age of the nanny and her relationship with their children made it feel more unsavory than the typical case of infidelity. Instead of using that fact to get emotional revenge, Eric used it strategically. The nanny resigned quickly and discreetly. Eric's wife was indebted to his silence and acknowledged privately that she needed counseling. He was able to keep his house, and his wife agreed he should be awarded primary care of the children.

In the end, those two wins were far more satisfying than publicly scandalizing the mother of his children, humiliating and creating a sense of betrayal in his children, and perhaps tainting the future of a young woman who wasn't quite mature enough to grasp the full impact of her own poor choice. Creating a scandal might have given Eric's ego a temporary win. In the end, however, he would have had to deal with the fact that he had dragged his children, as well as his STBX, through a devastating event that could not easily be overcome when his rage had subsided.

WISING UP: Think hard about what your public expressions of fault will do to your children, and how they will affect the divorce process. Loose lips sometimes can sink more than ships.

◇◇◇

The "I'm Out" Speech

I've seen a pattern by those who have already emotionally left the marriage when discussing their decision to leave:

I don't know what I'm doing any more. I need to find myself. Don't worry, I'll take care of you and the kids. Here, I've written out how everything will happen.

In other words, they've already processed the idea of going through a divorce, and they've come up with a plan for sharing this wonderful information in a way that they think will minimize the disruption, maybe even forestall the drama they dread.

If this is your speech, surprise! It doesn't work! Trying to ease the blow with these placating words and your plan for everyone else just doesn't work.

If you've thought of this pat solution for moving on, be warned that it is most likely just going to crank up the drama factor because you are tipping your hand.

And if your STBX doesn't see through your "just trying to find yourself" line, he or she will get to the truth eventually. When that happens, the drama factor is going to go through the roof because your STBX will now feel not only betrayed, but duped, as well.

So save yourself some grief. Dump the script. Face the mess you've made with honesty and integrity. And understand your perfect divorce plan may not be the plan that will work.

HITTING PAUSE

One of the tough things about launching the legal process of divorce is that you and your STBX are likely to be at different places, emotionally, on the pathway to ending the marriage.

The planner who has been thinking about divorce for a while or someone who has been miserable in the marriage for a long time is in a far different place from the person who is cooking dinner and finds out while the pot roast is burning that he or she is getting divorced.

These timing differences can impact the progress of the divorce. The planner, who may already have a new sweetie waiting in the wings, or who has run a spreadsheet outlining how everything gets divvied up, needs to realize that the other person has a lot of catching up to do.

The planner can't expect the other person to be right where he or she is.

If your spouse needs to catch up, you need to think about how long you've been planning and strategizing and considering your options. You may be surprised to realize that, wow, divorce as an option first came to you four years ago during that vacation where everything fell apart.

If you're the planner, understand that if you try to force your own vision of how this is going to go down onto your STBX before they have even had a chance to digest the fact that you've used the "D" word, you will likely be met with resistance. Even if you have a great plan, you're going to hit a brick wall.

Why? Because if you are the person who finally said this is it, there's some inherent distrust on other person's side. Even if you have both been miserable, if you are the one who says it, the other person feels betrayed. Maybe even embarrassed to be the one getting dumped.

So even your best ideas about temporary resolution run the

risk of being rejected. Your instinct, as the planner, may be to offer the reassurance that you've thought about it, and it's going to be fine. But the instinct of the ambushed spouse may be more along the lines of "you aren't getting off the hook that easily, and if you are offering me something, it can't be good." Your spouse's instinct may be to regain a little control by rejecting your ideas and coming up with ideas of his or her own—which may be very bad ideas born out of shock or fear or anger.

Whipping out the spreadsheet solution just makes it worse. Taking unilateral actions will be viewed as you being armed and ready for battle.

As the planner, you will want to be open and transparent, forthcoming with any information or documents your STBX spouse wants to see. This is part of rebuilding a bit of trust, which is going to be necessary to create a healthy strategic divorce.

Think about how long it took you to reach this conclusion, and understand that you'll need to give your spouse at least a fraction of that time to play catch up.

This doesn't mean waiting forever. Hitting pause doesn't have to be long-term. But recognize that your best settlement options lay in letting your spouse have a little space to catch up.

Good attorneys recognize this dynamic and should talk with you about it. If your attorney doesn't seem to understand and tries to pressure you to a place that will push your STBX over the edge, you may have a bad attorney. If that's the case, take the time your spouse is using to catch up with the situation emotionally to find a new attorney. If you don't, you may regret it before the divorce is over.

FEELING BLINDSIDED

Or you may be the one who has to catch up.

Stop. Breathe. Focus.

Your life has just been turned upside down. You don't get to choose to divorce or not. This horrible thing has been foisted upon you, and you have to go through it. You're going to be restructuring finances, resetting your emotions, maybe looking at a career change. Your family is going to look different. You'll be expected to redefine yourself. Whatever roles have been established for you within the family may not be the same. Your everyday routines will change. The ways you interact with your children won't be the same.

It's blindsided you. At least, that may be how it feels. It may feel sudden or unexpected and the very suddenness multiplies the trauma.

Your natural instinct in this situation may be to hunker down and wallow for a while. Please hear me: That's potentially one of the most dangerous things you can do. Be proactive, not reactive. You might be able to buy a little time, but you can't stop the progression of this divorce.

You can say you need a little time, but don't let time be a crutch. You have to do something with that time.

It's counter-intuitive when you want to lie in bed and cry all day, but start making lists of questions and concerns. Get ready. Use a counselor to get emotionally healthy. Find someone strong and upbeat and unwilling to condone your wallowing, someone who can gently nudge you out of your inaction.

If your area has divorce coaches or divorce assistants, hire one. A coach or assistant will help you with the business of divorce. Being with a person who is approaching this from a professional, strategic standpoint at this time will be far more valuable than friends who help by listening to you enumerate all the things you hate about your STBX. You're looking for someone who will help you walk through this stage of playing emotional catch-up respectfully, thoughtfully.

In fact, you want to avoid negative energy as much as possible during this time, and negative energy has a lot of different faces. Steer clear of friends with well-meaning advice about setting up your profile on Match.com—*let's show him!*—or going out to drown your sorrows night after night. These responses to your shock will not serve you well and can create situations that will come back to bite you during settlement negotiations or in the courtroom.

If you're wallowing, you're losing a strategic advantage. Allow yourself to grieve, but don't wallow.

Divorcing gracefully means recognizing how you should settle your case in a way that is less costly and avoids a trial. It means looking at divorce as a business decision and a blip in your life instead of the definition of the rest of your life.

Your actions at this time will also impact your children. Although it's hard, one of the worst things you can do is burst into tears when talking to your children. They're going to take cues from how you're dealing with this new development, and the level of trauma you're exhibiting will shape the level of trauma they feel.

During this fragile time, don't make any drastic decisions or agree to things you're not sure about. I've seen too many people who say, "OK, fine, we'll sell the house and get it over with," before they've even educated themselves about all their options.

What you're trying to do during this time is to call upon your best self, to find your stamina, your backbone, the qualities you call upon in other crisis situations. Really think about and identify those qualities in yourself and begin to plan.

Focus on what you need in order to get through the divorce—emotional support, legal information, financial information, and, yes, time to absorb this blow. Choose your experts, your advisors and your emotional supporters wisely, whether sounding-board friends, therapists or a lawyer.

You'll get through this. Give yourself permission to catch up instead of permission to fall down and stay down.

READY FOR THE REAL WORK

Wherever you fall in the spectrum of being prepared for the reality of divorce, the most important thing you can do is walk through it with great intentionality. Step by step, with the support of someone you trust to be wise and positive, ask yourself the following questions:

- What name can I give my emotions? Am I mad? Sad? Relieved? Afraid? What?

- Why are those my feelings? Where are they coming from?

- Where do I want to take my emotions from there? How do I shed any negative emotions and embrace this process?

When you've walked through all the emotions that come up when you answer these questions, you're ready for the real work of re-engineering your role in your family, with your children and with your STBX.

Old patterns aren't going to work any better in negotiating a deal during the divorce process than they worked during the marriage. Reliving and recreating your worst selves during the divorce process is not going to create a good divorce.

It's no party for the attorneys, either.

Instead, your goal needs to be to bring your best self to the divorce. That's how you get to the positive solutions that lead to a Wiser Divorce.

YOUR AUTHENTIC SELF

Sitting at the negotiation table with a divorcing couple sometimes calls to mind an image of two people sitting across the table with a bowl of potato chips between them. Each person starts digging into that bowl of chips, looking for all the ugly, broken chips, so they can take them out of the bowl and hurl them across the table at their STBX.

You never liked my family!

*Mother? You call yourself a **mother**?*

I can't believe I had children with you!

You cared more about your career … your clothes … your car than you cared about our family!

I can't believe you made me stop working!

Thanks to you, I've wasted the best years of my life!

You loser! Just tell me what I have to do to get you out of my life!

*You **never** made me happy!*

Let's be grown-ups, people! What does any of that have to do with the business of divorce? How is rehashing old grievances—which were sometimes just masking the real problems anyway—going to get us to a point of agreement about how to end the marriage successfully?

It won't. It can't. Childish bickering is not the most direct pathway to positive solutions.

One of the things I've learned in participating in hundreds of divorces is that some of the most explosive and unmanageable anger comes from years of people not having been their authentic selves. They hid who they were. They hid what was really starving or strangling them in the marriage. They hid what they really wanted and needed in the relationship. But now, at the end, it's time to stop dumping responsibility for your unhappiness onto the other person.

Be your authentic self. Your best self.

That's the first step in bringing your best self to the divorce. Also, when you bring your best self to the divorce, that's who you'll take with you into your Next Best Life.

◇◇◇

Aikido

I often tell clients to take the high road. This seems counterintuitive to many who are in the midst of divorce. A good friend described to me how the Japanese martial art of Aikido reflects this principle and teaches us a lot about divorcing successfully. Aikido is sometimes translated as "the way of harmonious spirit."

Aikido is performed not by resisting the moves of the attacker, but by blending with the motions of the attacker. Aikido redirects the force of the attack rather than opposing it head-on. This requires less physical strength than resistance.

In simple terms, when you push someone, your opponent uses your own energy to push back at you. When you push, the power against you actually builds instead of ebbing.

Think about this in your own divorce. Pushing negative energy at your STBX only strengthens their negative push back. Once you stop the push, your STBX is left with nothing to push back against. Usually this leaves them with nothing to attack, and many times it is their unraveling.

Use this high road approach to strategically enhance your negotiations and your trial outcome. And you will have more energy to focus on the positive parts of your life.

REHEARSING FOR YOUR NEXT BEST LIFE

What are the qualities that make you proud of yourself?

What actions and behaviors make you the kind of person others admire and look up to?

Are you willing to bring those qualities and behaviors to your divorce?

Maybe you pride yourself on being self-reliant, honest, and faithful. Maybe you're a good parent, a survivor, financially successful. Do friends say you're smart? Empathetic? A good listener? Optimistic? Does your life show signs that you can be strategic or visionary or calm in a crisis?

Whatever those wonderful qualities are, that's what you've got to bring to the divorce process.

You can, of course, resort to things you don't like in other people and don't like in yourself: being an emotional wreck, being dishonest, wanting revenge, ranting, being a controlling parent, spewing anger, dwelling in pessimism.

Crises typically bring out either the best or the worst in people. Our best traits get magnified. Or our worst characteristics become exaggerated. Divorce is one of those crises in which we reveal a lot about ourselves. *The manner in which we divorce reveals which is stronger in us, our best traits or our worst.*

How about it? Do you want to be a person you can be proud of? Or do you want to be the person you despise when you run into that person elsewhere in your life?

To bring your best self to the divorce, make a list of what you really like about yourself. Really. Write it down. Post it on the bathroom mirror. Make Sticky Notes for the dashboard of your car or the edge of your computer screen. Then make a commitment to bring that person to the table every time you're dealing with the business of your divorce. Every time you're interacting with your STBX. Every time you talk to your friends, family, and children.

Be that person, even if it's hard. Even if your STBX can't be his or her best self.

If you have a hard time with the idea of being nice during the divorce, remind yourself that *what you're doing is rehearsing for your Next Best Life.* You're practicing to be the person you want to be going forward.

I know you don't want to carry the bad marriage with you into the future. You want something better for yourself than to lug the residue of that marriage around with you for the next year, or five, or twenty.

It happens. Believe me. Some people carry the bitterness of their divorce to their death.

So how about it? Are you going to focus on the good waiting for you in the future? Are you going to focus on how blessed you are, because you married, that you now have these wonderful children who are the best thing that ever happened to you? Are you going to celebrate even the little victories, like the luxury of being able to read until midnight if you feel like it without somebody punching the pillow on the bed next to you? Can you look forward to drinking the milk straight out of the carton without feeling like a real pig, if that's what you want?

Or are you going to let whatever was bad in the past infect your future?

It's your choice. Your best self or your worst self?

If you start now making your best self a reality, you will be a healed and happy person by the time the divorce is over. And that's the ultimate definition of a Wiser Divorce.

EARNING "MOST LIKEABLE" POINTS

One thing I repeatedly have to tell people is how their actions will impact them if we have to go to court.

We've all heard about the person who wants a divorce, gets angry at the STBX and cuts off the credit cards or closes bank accounts. We know about people who party their way into oblivion, or have revenge-affair binges or engage in Jerry Springer-style tell-all behavior on Facebook.

◇◇◇

Playing Hide the Cash

Ashleigh's grandfather died shortly before she and her husband decided to divorce. Ashleigh's STBX said Ashleigh's grandfather had given her a lot of cash before he died; he wanted to know where that money went in case it should be factored into settlement negotiations.

Ashleigh told me, as her attorney, that her grandfather had given her the money to pay for his funeral expenses, and the money was gone.

The attorney for Ashleigh's STBX, of course, contacted the funeral home to verify this information. As it turned out, the funeral had been pre-paid years earlier.

Oops.

The cash, as it turned out, was in a safety deposit box. Ashleigh's grandfather had given her the money to start a college fund for her own children. But Ashleigh couldn't verify the source of the money, so it just looked like cash she had stashed away during the marriage that she would be required to divvy up with her STBX. By playing Hide the Cash, Ashleigh had just guaranteed that no court would believe it was a gift from her dying grandfather.

If Ashleigh had been honest with me, I could have told her that in our state, a gift from a family member does not have to be divided during a divorce. I could have helped her prove the gift before she lied, and safeguarded it for her children's college fund. Her lie about the money cost her and her children.

WISING UP: Lying or concealing information from your attorney is not a strategy; it is a big mistake.

That kind of behavior is not only potentially devastating to the children in the family, it is also childish and dumb. Think about it. If you end up in court in front of a judge who is going to be deciding your future, do you want the judge to look across the courtroom and see an immature, mean-spirited person? And believe me, even a year later, this kind of behavior is going to pop up in the documents the judge will be reviewing or come out in your testimony on cross-examination. During cross-examination, I've been able to get people to admit to behaviors as outrageous as lying earlier under oath (one was an attorney who was reported to the state bar by the judge, another was referred for a perjury prosecution), threatening in writing to slit my and my client's throats, installing spyware on my client's computer, or withholding information throughout the case. Who do you think ended up with the upper hand and more wins when the judge ruled?

So when you think about bringing your best self to your divorce, remember all the benefits:

- You get to feel better about yourself.

- You're rehearsing for the great future that's waiting for you.

- You're creating an environment where more choices can be made outside the courtroom, which always works in everyone's favor.

- You're potentially piling up "most likeable" points with the judge who may be hearing your case if you must have a trial.

This isn't to say that you can ever be 100 percent sure how a judge will react to your case. Judges are human, too, and as prone to misjudgment as any of the rest of us. You can read all about it in Chapter 9. But I have been through enough trials to know how judges typically react to people who bring their worst selves to the divorce process.

CHANGE THE RULES YOU PLAY BY

Having said this, it's entirely possible that your STBX will not be on the best-self bandwagon. You may be giving it your best shot to bring your best self to the divorce and still end up having to deal with STBX nightmare scenarios.

Some of the most difficult STBXs are:

- The Rich or Famous Big Shot

- The Abuser

- The "Taliban"

- The Mentally Ill/Addicted

- The Liar/Cheat

Most of these nightmare STBXs are out of touch with reality in some way. Most of them made the marriage difficult, and filing for divorce is not going to suddenly transform them into reasonable people.

But what you can do is refuse to be your own worst self just because that's the way your STBX plays the game. Even if that's what you've been reduced to in the marriage, divorce marks a new day. You can change the rules you play by, whether your STBX does or not.

Your challenge, if one of these STBXs is playing in the sandbox of your divorce, is to understand what you're dealing with, rely on your attorney to navigate the minefields, and tenaciously bring your best self to the table, no matter what your STBX throws at you. Because when you let a nightmare STBX dictate your emotions and your actions, you will lose.

Also, if you have to go to court, two unreasonable people won't impress a judge. But one will.

The only way to win in a battle with one of these nightmare

STBXs is to do what you can to break the patterns that were created during the divorce and bring your best self, with your best actions, to the table.

And by the way, if anyone has ever accused you of being one of these types, take a close look at yourself. It's never too late to begin cultivating your new best self.

Relationship patterns get magnified in an adversarial situation. Use this to your advantage, if it comes to this, by letting your STBX shoot him or herself in the foot. Taking the high road can be a great strategy when dealing with an STBX and an attorney who insist on getting down in the muck. If you can stop pushing and let the other person be who he or she is, this is often where success happens. Let the other party shoot themselves in the foot and see what happens once they are toeless.

STBX NIGHTMARES

Here's what to expect if you'll be dealing with the most problematic STBXs.

The Rich/Famous Big Shot: It's easy to feel that you're nothing when you have a very wealthy or well-known spouse. And if your STBX doesn't keep reminding you that you're nothing, someone else will.

I'll never forget the day I went to court with a client whose STBX was a high-profile celebrity. During a break, when the judge had gone to his chambers, the court clerk asked for the

STBX's autograph. Hero worship is a powerful force in our society today. Of course, my client felt no trial would be fair. I notified the judge about what had happened. The outcome of her case was ultimately fair. But if you are married to the rich or famous, ready yourself for the stars that may get in others' eyes, including the judge's.

You also have to be prepared for the fact that famous people often have a PR machine already in place. If the fight is going to be very public, the world that still worships the hero you are disenchanted with may see you as the bad guy in the story, the person who is trying to bring down their hero. Consult with your attorney and prepare a strategy.

A special caveat: *Be especially protective of your children if you're in the middle of a high-profile divorce.* Divorce is hard enough on kids without having to deal with notoriety.

Big Shots, whether they're rich or famous, have plenty of money to throw at their problems, as well. Sometimes they don't care how protracted the battle gets because they have deeper pockets than you do. The power balance shifts when one person holds a lot more money, and you can't just cry "no fair" and expect to have the scales balance again. You may be able to seek parity from the court by asking to have your attorney fees covered to even the scales, but even an adjustment by the courts can't fully correct the imbalance of divorcing a Big Shot.

Too many Big Shots are drunk on their own power. They are surrounded by "yes" men, people who do everything they say and cover for them if necessary. For Type A, narcissistic people, the world is their chess board—they are always calculating two moves to checkmate. They also like deal making, they like winning, and they like it when the rest of the world revolves around their every move.

It's better if you don't have to play the game, but if you do, your best bet is to have an attorney who is smart enough to play it for you. Then listen to that attorney. Do what they say.

One amazing woman I worked with was married to a big shot, well known in our state and nationally. We went to trial because his positions seemed totally unreasonable for the situation of their divorce. We got "starred"—the starstruck judge ruled in the big shot's favor and ignored the law. My client had the tenacity to go through a two-year appeal. She won. And established new legal standards in our state.

WISING UP: Don't wilt against the Big Shot STBX, but also know when and how to cut your losses.

The Abuser: You have to be willing to take steps to protect yourself and your children when you're getting out of an abusive situation, whether the abuse was physical or emotional.

You also have to make it an urgent priority to get healthy from the abuse. People who have been abused are broken and beaten down. They may not have the emotional reserves for a major battle during a divorce. Conversely, now that they are free, some people can become revengeful or unreasonable in an effort to right the suffering they have endured.

I represented one woman who just couldn't engage in the battle during her divorce because her marriage had been a battlefield for too long. She shared with me the physical, emotional, and sexual abuse she had endured. She had begun to cope by drinking too much. She was in emotional crisis. She couldn't take the ongoing litigation. For her own health, we agreed to things that wouldn't have been optimal, including the parenting schedule, in order to stop the stressful toll the ongoing litigation was taking on her.

After her divorce, she became healthy and strong. Ultimately, based on the abuser's continued behavior that was negatively affecting the children, we returned to court and adjusted the parenting schedule in a way that minimized the abuser's impact on the children. I am thrilled that she is now an advocate for other abused women.

Following abuse, how do you get to a place where you can make the right decisions for you and your children? Sometimes it takes years. Many times it takes therapy. It sometimes depends on who the abused person is at the core, how she or he grew up, how long the abuse has been going on, and how frequent it was. But you can and will recover.

The most important thing, if your STBX is an Abuser, is to get the right attorney. Some attorneys still don't recognize all the different forms of abuse or understand the cycle of abuse. The right attorney can shield you from further abuse during the divorce litigation because an Abuser often tries to continue the abuse through the divorce process. Abusers are often masters at finding attorneys who will partner with them, even if unconsciously, in that attempt. The Abuser will still try to control you, to intimidate you, even to harass you. Abusers may try to tap into your computer or follow you or make subtle threats that are easy to overlook for those who aren't familiar with patterns of abuse.

Again, you want an attorney who is attuned to that and is willing to be your champion and your buffer to minimize the possibility that litigation becomes a further tool of abuse.

The right attorney will also make sure you connect to other resources as you're getting out of an abusive relationship. You'll need someone who can help you make sure the terms of the settlement will be enforced. You'll want custody experts who understand that, just because an Abuser hasn't hit or threatened the children, his or her controlling behaviors and words can deeply affect a child's well-being. The lingering emotional aspects of abuse can have a major impact on children for years to come.

WISING UP: Divorcing an Abuser is delicate, and it can be dangerous. Look for an attorney who knows the territory, who can be sensitive to your situation and tough as nails with the Abuser. Forgive yourself if you aren't yet as strong as you will be.

* * *

The "Taliban": What do we know about members of the real Taliban? You cannot negotiate with them. They insist on absolute control. They won't listen to anything contrary to what they believe. They are unresponsive, unreasonable people. Figuring out why they do what they do is impossible because their motives and their beliefs are not rational.

What this means, for someone who is divorcing a "Taliban" spouse, is that settlement may be impossible because you can't negotiate with the Taliban. You can make yourself crazy if you try to figure out why Taliban spouses do what they do.

These divorces almost invariably end up in court, where the Taliban is often astounded—or outraged—to discover that the courts do not agree with their oppressive tactics. However, like many who can see only their own perspective, the Taliban may refuse to abide by the court's rulings. Taliban spouses seem willing to go to court indefinitely and spend whatever it takes to resist complying with divorce terms they don't believe in.

One of my clients was clearly entitled to receive spousal maintenance. She had not worked in more than twenty years, and her STBX, a Taliban spouse, made hundreds of thousands of dollars in the lucrative career he had built over the course of the marriage. We offered to settle for a reasonable amount early on. The Taliban refused. Throughout the case he asserted she was entitled to nothing, or almost nothing. No one, including his own attorney, could convince him otherwise. Off to court we went, and after months of expensive litigation, the court predictably ruled my client was entitled to spousal maintenance—in an amount higher than the last settlement offer we'd made.

Oh, and the Taliban had to pay my attorney fees.

WISING UP: Don't let the Taliban reign in your life. Sometimes your best option is to meet the Taliban head on. Trying to appease this type of STBX will get you nowhere; they simply cannot be appeased and believe in no other law or power than their own. Rely on your attorney for strength if this is your situation.

* * *

Mentally Ill/Addicted: Two important points to keep in mind when divorcing someone who is mentally ill or engaged in active addiction: 1) you may have to be the one who handles everything; and 2) a mentally ill or addicted person can be a danger to your children because he or she may be incapable of stepping up and parenting responsibly.

If you are divorcing a person in this category, you may find yourself motivated by sympathy for a STBX who is not fully capable of functioning in the world. Your tendency may be to rescue, to continue to be the caretaker, to shoulder too much of the burden going forward. Listen to your attorney, who can help you regain a perspective that isn't colored by too much sympathy for a person whose mental state can continue to bring you down even after everything is final, especially if there are children involved. Do what you need to do to keep your children safe, be it drug or alcohol testing, or keeping updated on your STBX's medications and treatment. You are entitled to this information when children are involved. Guard against regrets if the divorce finally forces them into appropriate treatment. It can and does happen.

WISING UP: Give up on a lost cause. You cannot solve the problems of an addicted or mentally ill person.

The Liar/Cheat: People experience a cheating spouse as the height of betrayal. It demoralizes the spouse who has been cheated on. Infidelity tends to cast doubt on everything else the cheating spouse has ever done or ever will do. Distrust taints everything. Has the whole relationship been a lie? Does the cheating spouse have hidden bank accounts? What other betrayals have occurred?

The cheating spouse, or even a spouse who has perpetuated lies during the marriage by secretly maxing out credit cards or hiding monetary gifts to friends or family, needs to understand that everything he or she does will be regarded with distrust. These spouses could give their STBX everything—100 percent— and it wouldn't be enough because the STBX would wonder what was still being hidden.

If your STBX cheated or lied, you have to separate those acts from the rest of what you know about the person. It doesn't mean everything was a lie in the entire marriage. Try your best to isolate these events into one "room" in your emotional house. It's hard, it's taxing, and the betrayal may be all you can think about. Remember, these behaviors are not about you.

My personal message to cheaters: You're responsible for this mess because you didn't have the guts to end an unhappy marriage without having someone else to run to. Take responsibility. Bend over backwards to make this right, knowing it's unlikely you'll ever fully be able to do so. Do it anyway. Apologize. Own your screw-up. Make concessions. Find your backbone.

Not many of us want to stay in a marriage with a liar or cheat. This is a hard life challenge, but it doesn't mean your next life won't be happy, and it doesn't mean you can't strategically divorce or bring your best self to the divorce. Sometimes you can even take advantage of the cheater's guilt to obtain more favorable settlement terms than you might otherwise get. At some point, most cheaters do feel remorse.

Also, don't reject a good settlement offer just because you are mad and distrustful. That move will end up only hurting you, not the cheater.

One of my clients had an epiphany and decided to disclose her affair to her husband to be honest in the marriage. At some level it was also to assuage her guilt. Her husband filed for divorce—no surprise. At the outset of the case, she told me to make a settlement offer so good that he couldn't say no. She was ready to swiftly pay, and pay big, for her transgression. Surprisingly, the STBX did say no because he had no trust in my client. After a year plus of litigation, he ended up with less than my client had offered and massive attorneys' fees in addition.

If you were the source of the dishonesty, disclose to your STBX whatever they legitimately want or need in order to feel comfortable with the divorce terms. If they want to look at the books of your business, let them. If they want to look at bank records, let them do that. Be ready to have everything you say and do in the divorce met with suspicion. Your honest efforts at this point to settle on reasonable terms may initially be rebuked. Deal with it. You created this scenario. So do whatever you must to create a good divorce and redeem yourself for multiplying the misery of ending a marriage.

Whichever end of the betrayal stick you're on, don't let it impact your children. Keep your mouth shut and the betrayal secret.

WISING UP: Expect betrayal to have an ongoing impact during the divorce. If you were betrayed, trust your attorney to discern the truths needed for you to make strategic divorce decisions. If you were the betrayer, know that everything you do or say will be met with suspicion. You've given up your right to be offended by that.

THE LESSER EVILS

When looking at who shows up at the divorce, there are lesser behaviors and attitudes that still have a negative impact on the process. Look for yourself here, be honest with yourself, and do what you can to overcome these actions in yourself. Above all, find an attorney who can help you mitigate these conditions if they show up in your STBX's behavior.

Absent clients: One of the things some people do to deal with divorce is not to deal. This may be especially true for the person who has the divorce forced on them. Not dealing—or being passive aggressive—is an attempt to make this divorce business to go away. Your best divorce is one you participate in.

Here's what an absent client looks like. The attorney says I need so and so, and the Absent Client just doesn't comply. When information about the divorce shows up in the mail or email, the Absent Client doesn't look at it. The Absent Client doesn't keep up and doesn't understand what's going on—there's a total lack of self-education.

This degree of disengagement can significantly impact the ability to settle because one of the parties is just not dealing.

Recently one of my clients came to me two years after we settled her divorce. She wanted to know why we had agreed to certain terms. She thought we had missed this detail or that detail of the situation, which we hadn't. She was now upset and mad. The truth: She had withdrawn from the divorce. She had disappeared. Despite my communications with her, she just wasn't into it and was not following the details of her own divorce, even though we discussed the details face-to-face, and she acted like she understood. She had disappeared, then woke up two years later and couldn't figure out why she got what she got, even though what she got was good. She had to spend extra money with us to recreate her divorce, so she could be assured she had received what she should have received.

Adrian Monk: Remember the OCD TV detective who could perceive and connect details no one else attached any significance to? Some clients need to know and discuss, in painstaking detail, how and why every single move in their divorce is made. Every detail gets second-guessed. Every pleading, every letter, every communication has to be scrutinized under a microscope and explained.

That's okay if that's what you want. This certainly can be part of my job. It is, however, going to cost you more in attorney fees. It's also going to slow down the entire process. It really gets you nowhere to argue with your attorney about the laws that apply to your divorce when they are explaining them to you, either. If you have that level of distrust in your attorney, get a new one.

It's good to be engaged. It's good to understand what's happening. But you hired an attorney who will never be able to convey to you in the short time of your divorce their vast knowledge of the law, the instincts they have developed over years of practice about how to present your case, or every law, rule, and case that impacts your divorce. Try to accept that having something explained again and again is not going to change the outcome.

As Monk often said, paying attention to the details can be a blessing—and a curse. Educating yourself is good. Trying to always second guess the expert you hired to help you may not be good—for you or for them or your case.

The Obstructionist: Surprisingly, some of the worst Obstructionists are attorneys.

There are the attorneys who tell their clients that certain outcomes will never happen in court, so they shouldn't compromise. Whether they are right or not matters less than their adamant insistence that their clients should litigate and fight and refuse to compromise. Their refrain is, "This won't happen in court, so don't do it."

For these attorneys and their clients, negotiating a strategic settlement is not about the emotional economy of staying out of court. It isn't even about whether the client can afford the terms of a compromise—could perhaps even save money by sidestepping months or years of litigation. For Obstructionists, it's all about winning.

Or, to the eternal shame of the profession, it's all about squeezing the maximum in legal fees out of a client.

If you find yourself working with an attorney who keeps telling you no judge will make a certain decision so why should you compromise, it may be time to cut your losses and find new representation.

Clients, of course, can be Obstructionists too. It can take the form of hiding information from their attorneys forever (or until the other side finds it) or until the client thinks it's time for the attorney to know. Or it can mean refusing to negotiate at all, refusing to see the positives and negatives of their position because they feel they are right. Obstructionism will get you nowhere, and usually will harm you.

The Victim: Some people truly have been traumatized, oppressed and repressed in a marriage. People who have been physically, mentally, or emotionally abused are a good example. Others just feel that the divorce is not fair, that the laws are not fair, and darn it, they are victims in this unholy action called divorce.

When you decide to use the divorce as the opportunity to punish your STBX, or wallow in the unfairness of it all, the chance for divorce to become an instrument of healing goes out the window. For these people, divorce needs to be seen as the pathway to freedom, not the direct route to retribution. They need to get over "fair" because there's really no such thing in life. Really. "Fair" is not a legal concept you can achieve in your divorce, or that your attorney can achieve for you, or that a court may be able to give you. Take the words "it's not fair" out of your vocabulary right now.

The only way to be free is to refuse to continue living in the Victim role.

BEST-CASE SCENARIO

Divorce can feel like the worst-case scenario. It isn't. The worst-case scenario is the bad marriage that keeps going and going and going—the Energizer Bunny of bad relationships that just won't quit.

So if divorce becomes the next step for your marriage, the best-case scenario is for you accept the inevitable and bring your best self to the table.

When you can do that, you simplify the process, you save time, money and emotions, and you contribute to the likelihood of a Wiser Divorce. You set yourself up for leaving behind all the old patterns and creating new patterns going forward, so you can truly be your best self in your best new life—including a new relationship, when the time is right.

6 Attract Good Communication Karma

Poor communication always, *always* contributes to a broken marriage. Healthy communication always, *always* creates good karma for your divorce.

A strategic divorce calls for healthy communication in three areas: how you talk to your STBX and your children; transparency with your attorney; and minimizing negative dialogue with friends, family, and acquaintances, both face-to-face and online. Yes, even divorce is not immune to the impact of social media.

REPAIRING THE COMMUNICATION BREAKDOWN

You will have to communicate with your STBX.

Rarely is an ex out of your life completely just because he or she has packed up and moved out of the house. This is certainly true when there are children. But even when there are no children, it is rare that two people can disentangle their lives without some kind of conversation. There is shared property to be disposed of or divided. Maybe a business asset must be preserved or protected, requiring a degree of civility or even collaboration. Separating finances calls for some level of cooperation.

In fact, navigating a strategic divorce may call for more communication than you've done in years.

Of course, if you could communicate successfully with your STBX, divorce might not be in your future. People who communicate well have a better chance of staying in the marriage. So I predict that if you are getting divorced, somewhere along the way, communication broke down, along with everything else—the sexual relationship, the sense of being partners and friends, the interests or hobbies you shared. Most of that you can and will let go of during a divorce. The time for repairing them is over.

If you can begin to repair the communication breakdown—if you build some good communication karma—you have a chance of salvaging a good divorce from the wreckage of a bad marriage. If you can't, the whole process is going to be much more difficult than it needs to be.

Communication issues sometimes reflect other things that messed up the marriage. Everything that was broken about the marriage impacts the way two divorcing people speak to each other. The unspoken things suddenly surface, dying to be said now that there's a sense the damage has already been done.

I promise you, the damage that can be done during a divorce can be just as painful and just as long-lasting as the damage done during the disintegration of the marriage.

THREE QUESTIONS

Remember the importance of thoughts, words and actions? Communication is about all three. Communication starts with our thoughts, gets translated into words, and its nuances are conveyed in our actions.

Seeing Yourself Clearly

An inability to communicate in a clear, unemotional manner can have drastic negative consequences on the outcome of your divorce.

William was going through an emotionally taxing divorce and custody battle. His wife Jeanie was taking the position that he was incapable of parenting their children as well as she parented them, primarily because she was angry about his emotional absence in their marriage. Her position was that his parenting time should be strictly limited, which meant a formal custody evaluation would get underway.

William was so upset about Jeanie's unreasonable position that despite his usual professional and rational demeanor, every phone call with Jeanie was five times longer than it needed to be–which meant William usually ended up delivering a rant of some kind. His emails, also five times longer than necessary, read suspiciously like a rant as well. When William and I were face to face or in a room with his STBX, he always came across as, well, a little unhinged.

And he wasn't. Except when it came to Jeanie.

His frustration only fueled Jeanie's belief that he was not emotionally capable of proper parenting.

I suggested William hire a communication coach, so he could break this pattern, which was feeding into Jeanie's position, and so he could communicate to the custody evaluator without anger or blame.

Finally, William agreed to meet with a communication coach. The coach suggested videotaping a session so William could observe how he looked and sounded when he talked about Jeanie and his children.

William's coach and I both knew that if William came across as irrational and angry, his valid points about his bond with his children and his ability to parent them lovingly would be discounted not just by Jeanie and her attorney, but by the custody evaluator as well. And angry men don't play well in court.

After viewing the videotape, William experienced an epiphany. He understood, finally, how he looked and sounded. He realized his communication focus should be on himself and his children and what he offered as a parent, rather than on why Jeanie's position was wrong and his anger about what she was putting him through. He at last saw the truth and was able to break his old patterns of communication in time for the custody evaluation, which led to a custody report recommending he have equal time with his children.

WISING UP: You help your case when you focus communication on your own positives and not your STBX's negatives.

Healthy communication starts with your thoughts, which is why we launched into the discussion of creating a good divorce by suggesting that we do everything we can to banish negativity. If we're full of negative thoughts and emotions, there is no way to keep that negativity—anger, hatred, bitterness, blame, contempt, vindictiveness—out of our communication with a STBX. Our thoughts are revealed in the words we choose, in our tone of voice, in how we hold our body, in micro-expressions that almost everyone can read instinctively. Even if we can't name what we're seeing, we feel it, we internalize it, and we react to it. Then we just as instinctively project it back to the person we've received it from.

And suddenly we've gone from healthy communication to combative communication.

Even if you've made a commitment to banishing negativity, intense emotions make it so easy to say the wrong thing. To let something hurtful slip out. To stumble around and say something you don't mean, even. So we need to *think* about what we want to say, and how we want to say it. This is true about conversations with the STBX and it is especially true about conversations with children.

For those difficult conversations we know will come up, I strongly recommend a practice of scripting. Start by asking yourself these questions:

- What exactly do I want to say?
- What do I *not* want to say?
- What inflammatory language do I want to avoid?
- How can I keep the conversation brief to minimize the chance that the conversation will take a wrong turn?

One thing I hear a lot, for example, is that people don't want to see or speak with their STBX when they are exchanging the kids. Wisely so. This is a situation that can be fraught with intense emotions. It's a reminder that our relationship with our children is inevitably changing as we change the relationship with their other parent. It's a reminder that we'll be without our children more than we're used to. Lonely, possibly. And the wrong words in front of children can harm them forever.

So write a simple script.

Have a great time!

I hope you had a nice time with the kids. See you next week!

Not: *You're five minutes late bringing the kids back! What did you feed the kids?*

Or, when speaking to the children, *What time did you go to bed? Was anyone else with you except Dad?*

Questions like these could easily go unsaid and invite information you may not really want or need. It can even make you look nosy or intrusive in circumstances where it's so much easier to assume the negative than it is to assume the positive.

Another example of an opportunity for dangerous conversation can be if a STBX raises an issue about settlement terms with you privately, outside the presence of your attorney. There's the danger of agreeing to something you'll wish you hadn't or making a revelation you might regret. It's best to have your script for this situation, stick to that script, and don't allow yourself to be pulled into further discussion. Have your little speech ready.

I'm really going to think about what you said, but I want to get my attorney's feedback before I respond.

Stick with that. Relentlessly stick with that. If your STBX tries to press you for more or continue the conversation, repeat what you've said. Repeat it calmly and pleasantly. Stay in that neutral territory. Whatever you do, don't let the conversation break down into, "Well, I just think you're trying to …"

Just pretend every single call or conversation is being recorded, and ask yourself what the judge would think if she heard what you're about to say or saw this text or email you're about to send. Believe me, attorneys bring these wish-I-could-take-them-back moments to court all day long.

DIALING BACK THE HOSTILITY

One of my clients could not figure out how to stay in an emotion-free zone during her communications with her STBX. She had learned, as many people do, that emailing or texting on significant matters could lead to miscommunication, both because important details were missed or misconstrued and because nuances of tone and attitude got lost. But when it came to oral communication, emotions too easily got in the way.

My client and I talked about the situation and came up with a solution. When she and her STBX needed to stay neutral, they agreed to meet in a restaurant or coffee shop. The very public arena kept them aware of their tone of voice, the volume of their voices, and how others at nearby tables might hear them. They managed to dial back significantly on the hostility because they had to at least behave politely. It changed their dialogue, and over time it changed how they felt about each other, and ultimately, it changed their ability to reach agreements both could live with.

If for some reason face-to-face meetings are out of the question, and emailing is going to be your primary mode of communication with your STBX, keep your writing to the point. Keep emotions out of it. Don't write long paragraphs about why you are right and your STBX is wrong. If you can't seem to stop yourself, have your attorney review your emails before you send them until you can follow the rules on proper and effective communication.

Smile. Smile even if you don't feel like smiling. Smile at your STBX. Smile at your STBX's attorney. Smile at your own attorney. Smile at the judge. Nothing creates good communication karma like a smile. And it will change your attitude for the better.

I coached one of my clients to pretend her STBX was a cousin she talked to only once or twice a year at holiday gatherings. A nice enough cousin to whom she would be polite and exchange pleasantries, but with whom she had no emotional investment. Once she started emailing her STBX as her "cousin," her communications drastically improved and the negativity disappeared.

So no matter what your method of communication, keep it neutral. Keep the topic focused. Keep it simple.

This applies when you're talking to the children, as well. In Chapter Seven you'll find more detail about interactions with children during a divorce. For now, just keep in mind that children basically need to know their lives won't be horribly disrupted. They don't need details, they need reassurance.

You don't need to worry about a thing. Mommy and Daddy will both always take care of you. We're going to work everything out, and you're going to be fine. We're all going to be fine.

And by the way, when you hear yourself saying those words to your children, believe them yourself.

TRANSPARENT COMMUNICATION

Your attorney can help create the dynamics of healthy communication by setting the stage for the right degree of transparency during negotiation, mediation or collaborative divorce. Transparency with the other side begins with transparency in your communications with your attorney.

To achieve a successful strategic divorce, you have to lay out all the cards for your attorney. If you try to withhold any information from your attorney because you think it will hurt you, let me assure you: Withholding it will hurt you. One way or the other, the information you try to hide will hurt you.

On the other hand, a good attorney can make all the cards, positive or negative, work for you.

Most people have seen enough movies or TV to know about attorney-client privilege. The average person thinks that means your attorney can't disclose anything you tell him or her, period. Attorney-client privilege is not absolute. In a divorce, your attorney may be required to disclose certain things. Your attorney can't hide things that are material to the case—things like hidden money or mental health issues in custody cases. They will either have to disclose it or get out of your case.

What Dating Can Get You

About online dating during a separation or during settlement negotiations: Don't. And doing it before you even tell your spouse you want a divorce? Downright stupid.

Emily and Jason were looking like a model couple, as far as divorcing people go. They weren't fighting or badmouthing each other during mediation. They had adjusted well to co-parenting during the process. They had agreed on several significant compromises. Signing of the final settlement papers was days away.

Then Jason's friend told him about Emily's on-line dating profile. Turns out she'd had her son take her profile picture, which was very suggestive.

Jason went off the deep end. The whole settlement agreement fell apart. Not because he wanted to stay with Emily, but because she had involved their son in something that seemed inappropriate for a child. Not to mention that her behavior so soon after separating felt like a slight to their years of marriage, and he himself certainly felt emotionally nowhere near the point of dating.

It took months to reach the next agreement. The costs associated with the divorce went way up, money taken right out of their pockets. This round of negotiations was not nearly as pretty as the first round.

I'm not saying it's wrong to date during your divorce. I'm not saying you're a bad person if you post a profile on an online dating site. I'm just saying it's a great way to have things blow up in your face. That emotion-free zone comes to an end in a hurry under circumstances like that.

WISING UP: If you must date, do it quietly, circumspectly. Don't flaunt it in your STBX's face.

An affair, on the other hand, is not typically considered material to divorce negotiations. I know, infidelity may feel extremely material if it's happened to you. Most divorces are no-fault, and a cheating spouse just doesn't enter into the equation.

The important thing is that you should not be the one deciding what's material, and what's relevant. Let your attorney do his or her job. Let your attorney determine what must be disclosed and when to disclose it and how to weave it into the narrative of your divorce in the most advantageous way.

Otherwise, you run the risk of having it blow up in your face. A good attorney can help you avoid that.

COOPERATIVE COMMUNICATION

The starting point for healthy communication in a strategic divorce is to find points of consensus at the outset. Even in the most horrible cases, divorcing people can usually find something they can agree to, even if it's as inconsequential as who's going to take the couch. Maybe you can agree whether to list the house for sale or not. Or who gets which car or where the dog's going to live. In a simple face-to-face meeting, it's usually possible to find a few points both parties can agree on.

One good way to get to a place of healthy communication is to agree to cooperate for the sake of the children. Can you agree to filter every decision through the prism of whether it will be in the best interests of the children? For the sake of the children, can you agree to say "please" and "thank you," even if you start out thinking you hate your STBX's guts?

Another starting point for cooperative communication is for everybody to list what documents and information they feel they need in order to resolve settlement issues. This includes a commitment from both attorneys to cooperate in providing back-and-forth information. Most states today have mandatory disclosure laws, but an attorney still has the power to make the process easier and more cooperative or to drag the process out, increasing the aggravation factor in the process.

And don't take significant unilateral actions during the divorce process. That really messes up the ability to have good communication. Doing things like getting counseling for the children without telling your spouse, cancelling insurance, selling automobiles, emptying bank accounts, or making expenditures of large sums beyond what is necessary for day-to-day life will only lead to distrust and more attorneys' fees.

CHOOSE YOUR CONFIDANTS WISELY

The more you say something, the truer it becomes and the more it gets ingrained in your head.

When it comes to divorce, one of the most common reactions is this natural instinct to talk, talk, talk, talk, talk. To tell it to our six best girlfriends over designer martinis. To gripe on the way to a ball game with the guys. To relive everything to everyone. You have to be cognizant that how much you talk, as well as how and what you talk about, will impact your thoughts about your divorce.

One of the first instincts in the early days of realizing a divorce is in our future is to begin to rally the troops behind us. It's as if everyone has been infected with this need to create the right spin by getting out in front of the story, making sure the people in our personal circle know we are right and the other person is wrong.

Having witnessed this too many times, I no longer need to ask if it is in anyone's best interests to be supported in the "I'm right and my STBX is a jerk" campaign. Is it best for you? Best for the children? Best for the outcome of the divorce? No. No, it isn't.

First, let's remember that our goal is to reinforce our own *positive* thinking. We want to get our own heads wrapped around the idea that getting a divorce will mean some changes, and we intend to make those changes as positive as possible. So what good does it do to keep wading through the bad stuff with friends and family and coworkers and the dental hygienist you only see twice a year? The negative messaging of disparaging your STBX to the world becomes a snowball rolling down a hill.

The way you act when you are in the middle of a divorce becomes the way your friends and family react, which affects their ability to truly support you during this major life transition. They and you become consumed not with successfully navigating the process, but with *she did this* or *I'm right* or *he's evil*. Focusing on personality instead of strategy seriously hampers your ability to achieve a Wiser Divorce.

Second, your communication to your personal network during your divorce is going to impact your relationship with all these people down the road. You may think your friends and family want to hear all about Divorce Hell day in and day out. They do not. They will get sick of it. They will wonder when you are going to be fun and normal again.

I still clearly recall, all these many years later, discussing my possible divorce again and again and again with a friend who finally said to me: "Angie, we're not going to talk about this anymore. Either do something about it or stop talking to me about it." My friend was right. Talking and talking about my bad marriage was not good for me and not good for my friendships. And it wasn't changing anything.

When having that self-control gets hard, and you're tempted to vent and vent and vent, call to mind someone you know who has gone on *ad nauseam* during their divorce. The ones who can't talk about anyone else or anything else, and believe this: Your divorce is not different. People will react to you the same way.

Third, the things we say—especially the negative things—spread poison. We think, *I'll talk to his sister; she's on my side.* Then the extended family soon becomes like a glass of water. That one drop of negativity infects everybody. That is bad communication karma.

Bottom line, let only a few of your very closest friends and family in on your angst, if you must. Choose wisely who will be your confidants. If you share your angst with everyone else you know or are acquainted with, they may start to think you're as crazy as you sometimes feel in the middle of a divorce. There's nothing adult about that. This is not bringing your best self to the table. In the end, you'll find yourself needing to recover your image and your relationship with some of the people whose respect you most want.

So your communication strategy for the world at large is to be thoughtful about whom you talk to and circumspect about what you say about your divorce.

CHANGING YOUR DIVORCE DYNAMIC

To be sure you're telling the story that you want to become your truth, post-divorce, remember the technique of scripting. It can be especially important to set the tone from the beginning, when you're announcing the news to family and close friends. It's so temping to say, "I'm totally sick of him." Or "I'm done with her."

Instead, what if you said, "I'm really sorry to tell you that Mary and I are getting a divorce. I know you've always liked her, and I hope you'll continue to have a good relationship with her."

If friends or family members want to talk to you about your divorce, they might say how sorry they are, or what a jerk your STBX is. How will you respond? By bringing them into your drama? By acknowledging your life is now ruined? Or will you change your divorce dynamic by saying, "Of course we are disappointed our marriage will be ending, but Bob is a good parent to our children, and I am not going to speak rudely of him or let others do so."

What are you going to say, think, and do from the starting point of your divorce forward? You can emphasize everything negative, or you can decide to minimize the negativity and the gossip. Of course you will and should confide in your closest friends and family about how you may be feeling. But the purpose of that is for you to personally find strength and guidance, which is positive. It is putting negativity on every aspect of your divorce that is unhealthy.

A script that becomes your party line throughout the divorce will also come in handy with people who express their concern or ask questions during the divorce. Some of them may be genuinely concerned. Others may just enjoy being the one who is in the know. Either way, do you really want to have every other parent at school or everyone in the office know your personal life details and challenges? Remind yourself how you want to sound and what information you want to convey when people ask you questions. You may even want to have a conversation with your STBX about your desire, and hopefully his or hers, to manage the way the world perceives your divorce, especially if there are children.

Instead of, "You won't believe how bad it is (or what she's done)" when someone asks, think about how differently the world will perceive your divorce if your standard response to queries, kind or otherwise, is, "Thank you for asking. We're trying to do this the best way we can for the kids."

And when your best pal tries to commiserate by saying, "OMG, you must hate him!" that's your opportunity to say, "No, I'm not going to hate him. I'm going to take a totally different action."

Even if you don't feel that way but tell people that you're not going to play the blame game, or that you're focused on making this easier for the children and want everyone's support in doing so, can you imagine how the tone of any gossip might change?

With the words you choose, it's possible to change the whole dynamic around your divorce. That's good communication karma. And it reinforces positive solutions.

KEEPING YOUR DIGNITY

The ways we communicate to the world about our divorce are no longer limited to the people we encounter and talk to face to face or on the phone. Today, we live our lives online. That includes our divorces.

We text it. We turn it into a status update on Facebook. Our lives are out there in blogs, on Instagram, on Twitter. Personally, I don't want people knowing everything about my life but apparently I am increasingly in the minority.

It's not necessary to tell everyone the nitty gritty details of your divorce. If you are going to act with dignity in your divorce, part of that is how you communicate and to whom you communicate. Using social media to communicate about divorce lowers the level of dignity a notch or two. Really, how does it help for your entire community of Facebook friends or Twitter followers to know the details, even if you're keeping it positive?

If you think it's going to make you feel better to badmouth your STBX, keep this in mind: When you share it online, it's not only out there forever; you have no control over who may end up seeing it. I don't care what your privacy settings are. If you put it

Social Media, Divorce and Safety

If you use Facebook, you're essentially allowing people to stalk you. That may be fairly innocuous most of the time. But if your stalker includes a STBX with anger issues or a history of violence, you could be compromising your safety and the safety of your children.

Suppose you "check in" and say you're having dinner at a certain restaurant. Your STBX could show up and make your life miserable. A certain kind of STBX might decide it's the perfect time to grab the kids and run.

It may seem innocent enough. But ask yourself if it's really worth the risk just so you can feed the curiosity of your cyber community.

online there's every chance that your co-workers, your children's friends' parents—or your children—will see it at some point. That has led some states to curtail a parent's right of free speech on social media in favor of "protecting" children.

Not only can the misuse of social media harm your children, but anything you post online can come back to bite you in the courtroom.

I see it every day. People sabotage themselves with what they put on social media. People ask for more money for spousal maintenance because they are disabled and can't work, but create a dating profile that says they like to take long hikes or go skiing, information that can be verified by private investigators. *Your STBX's attorney will look for this information and will share it with the judge and it can adversely affect your case*—not to mention costing you more in attorney fees.

You want shared custody of your young children but can't resist posting that cute photo of your inebriated self or a photo of you and your new love interest getting affectionate. *Your STBX's attorney will look for this information and will share it with the judge and it can adversely affect your case.*

Your STBX hopes to take you to the cleaners and you're trying to prove that the business you own isn't worth as much as it was during your marriage. Yet your company website boasts (not entirely truthfully) that your business has been number one in its field the last five years running. Anything you post online potentially gives the other side real evidence to use against you. *Your STBX's attorney will look for this information and will share it with the judge and it can adversely affect your case.*

It's simple. Here's Angie's Rule: **Refrain from posting online details about your divorce, your STBX or any topic that could impact your divorce.** That's not a suggestion. It may seem restrictive. But it's a common-sense rule for good divorce in this day and age.

We don't take seriously enough the role social media plays in divorces today. Anything you post online, whether on your business website or a personal blog or your Tweets or your LinkedIn profile, can be accessed. It happens in divorces every day. Every single thing you do during your divorce is going to be looked at by the other side. Anything that shows up online can backfire.

Your need to proclaim to the world that your wife is bad or your new boyfriend is hot may come across to a judge as unsavory; a judge may feel that it says something critical about your judgment or your credibility. Judges are human and may very likely decide that if you have poor judgment in one area, you may lack good judgment in another area of your life. While it's impossible to know to what degree a judge is impacted by liking or not liking a person in court, human nature—and my professional experience—tells me it can and does happen.

Social Media, Divorce and Privacy, Part 2

Did you know that in most states it is against the law to destroy potential evidence in a lawsuit, including deleting an email or a text or a Facebook post that could be used to incriminate you or influence a judge's opinion in any way?

When it comes to cyber evidence, there's no prohibition against incriminating yourself.

In addition, if your spouse knows your passwords, it is often not considered an invasion of privacy for your STBX to gather up information from your texts and emails in the privacy of your own home. So if you are, for whatever reason, still sharing a house during the divorce process, remember that you have no assumption of privacy.

If you're not yet paranoid about how shaky your privacy is online, here's something that should cinch it for you: In one of my cases, for the mere price of $50, the STBX sent my client an email that, when opened, enabled him to see every key stroke my client made on her computer.

Be safe, not sorry, when it comes to privacy online: Assume there's no such thing.

CELEBRATING GOOD KARMA

A lot of things change when we go through a divorce. Initially, many things seem destined to change for the worst. We may lose our house. We may have less income. We may be spending less time with our children—and they may be hurting because of our actions. We may find ourselves on the outs with our in-laws, even if we've had a great relationship before. We may find our circle of friends shrinking, depending on who gets custody of what relationships.

Over time, most of those things will heal and we'll find positive fall-out from the divorce—but it will take time.

One of the positive changes, and one we can intentionally create, is becoming a better communicator. We can even change bad communication patterns in existing relationships. That's a change that will pay off every day, in every relationship, for the rest of our lives. Even at a time when we seem to be grieving so many things, good communication karma is something we can begin to celebrate right now. What you put out will come back to you, good or bad.

7 Put the Kids First

The decision to divorce started with you or your spouse. Your kids did not make this decision. Yet every part of their lives will be disrupted to a greater or lesser degree by this decision to change the only life they've known.

This isn't a reason not to divorce, if divorce is the only way to create a happy, healthy future for yourself and your children. *Your* emotional health inevitably affects *their* emotional health. This is simply a call for you to place your children's needs first in your thoughts, your words and your actions throughout the process. If you do this, your children will come through divorce in a better place than they were in during a miserable marriage.

If you don't do this, your children can wind up being an emotional mess. And you will be partly to blame.

Oblivious and self-absorbed parents can't read the signs that their children are hurt and traumatized. If someone in your child's life tells you that your child needs help, don't reject their input. Accept it and act on it. Right away.

WHO ARE YOU REALLY THINKING ABOUT?

Let's start with your thoughts.

How are you thinking about your children as you move toward divorce? Are you thinking about how your relationship with them may change? Maybe you're thinking about how much you'll miss them when they're spending weekends or summers with your STBX. It wouldn't be unusual to find yourself very anxiously thinking about how you're going to survive, what you're going to do with your life, when they're gone for days or weeks. Or how you'll manage to stay sane thinking about whether they will like your STBX's new significant other more than they like you. If you're like some parents I see, you're even thinking a lot about how you can make sure your kids know who the bad guy is in this sad situation.

Does any of that sound familiar?

Then hear this: *You aren't thinking about your kids. You're thinking about yourself.*

That's right. You're consumed with how this divorce is going to change your role in their lives, not about how you can minimize the impact of divorce on them. Grow up! It's time to begin to separate your feelings of loss from what's best for your children. It's time to look at what your children need.

You are probably picking up a certain edginess in me right now. Divorcing parents who don't place their kids' needs first really tick me off.

WHO SHOULD WIN? THE KIDS

Priority one for divorcing parents: Your kids come first.

Not the new girlfriend. Not the house. Not the money. Not revenge. Not proving who's right and who's wrong. Not shame or blame or rallying allies. Not getting the kids on your side. Your kids come first.

When I say that, I don't mean in the sense of who wins the custody battle. Here's who should win the custody battle: *Your kids*. That's right. Custody decisions aren't about who gets the most days with the children. Custody decisions are about deciding what's best for the children. If they have two loving parents, they need to continue to have frequent and meaningful experiences with both of them.

By the way, financial decisions should be about what's best for the children, too. I can't tell you how many immature, vengeful adults I've seen during my years litigating divorce who want to make their STBXs suffer financially—cutting off credit cards or bank accounts, yanking the rug out from under their economic security and stability—with absolutely no regard for whether their children's lives will be disrupted by their petty, selfish actions.

Recently at a settlement meeting, my client's STBX announced that he would not agree for his twin daughters to continue in ballet lessons, even though they occurred only during my client Joyce's parenting tine. If he didn't agree, Joyce would have to foot the bill by herself, which she could not afford to do. The girls had taken ballet for years and were in the midst of preparing for their year-end recital. A recital he had always proudly attended. In fact, he regularly bragged to his friends about the girls' solos and talent.

I wanted to smack him. But I'm a professional, so I managed to ask, "Do you not have the money to pay for ballet?"

I knew the answer to that, of course. I had all his financial records. He had plenty of money. My client didn't.

"I'm not going to pay for ballet until Joyce agrees to the spousal maintenance my attorney says the judge will give her," he said, cutting his eyes in my client's direction to enjoy her reaction to his power play.

I counted to ten. Joyce, to her credit, appeared to be doing the same. Joyce had been schooled on staying in an emotion-free zone, even if her STBX had not.

"Tell me about your daughters," I said after we'd all had a moment. "How do they like ballet?"

The first hints of discomfort crept onto his face.

He didn't seem to have a ready answer, so I continued.

◇◇

Top 10 Ways to Screw Up Your Kids

1. Speak poorly of the other parent or let others speak poorly of the other parent in the presence of your children. Be careless about letting them overhear your conversations with others about your divorce.

2. Tell them why you're getting divorced. Extra points for gory details.

3. Argue about the divorce with the other parent in front of them. Heated discussions count, too.

4. Tell them details about your divorce litigation or show them the letters or pleadings in your divorce. Another good opportunity for gory details.

5. Ask them who they want to live with. Less effective in screwing them up, but still a nice touch to increase their confusion and guilt, is to ask them their preference about the parenting schedule.

6. Use them as a go-between to communicate messages to the other parent. Feeling the pressure of being in the middle of feuding parents is a great strategy for creating a dysfunctional childhood.

7. Tell them you do not have money to do or buy the things they want because the other parent isn't paying you.

8. Tell them you will miss them or that you're sad without them when they spend time with the other parent. Guilt is good. Work this one for all it's worth.

9. Grill them about what they did at the other parent's house. Especially if there's a new significant other.

10. Incessantly call, email, or text them when they are with the other parent.

"Would your daughters like to stay in ballet? What do they have to say about your decision?"

Of course, neither he (nor apparently his attorney) had thought about the children. They were focused on the chess board, calculating the string of moves to checkmate.

During that discussion it was decided that Joyce and her STBX would do something radical (at least in divorce war): They would talk jointly to their daughters about their ballet classes. In the end, both children expressed they loved ballet and didn't want to quit. Having spoken to his daughters directly, Joyce's STBX realized his error in punishing the children to extract settlement concessions from Joyce. He continued to pay for ballet.

If you have children, your children come first. That requires a degree of discernment and selflessness that reveals all the gamesmanship of divorce as petty and immature. It requires abandoning your selfishness.

Before you pat yourself on the back because you're all about your kids, keep reading. Maybe you're doing everything right. Maybe you're not.

FEELINGS OF LOSS

Deciding who will have the kids when and who will make decisions for them can be an all-out war.

Sometimes it's about doing what is clearly and easily best for the kids. One parent is an addict or an abuser or mentally ill, or just so emotionally or physically unavailable that co-parenting or sharing parenting time in some kind of equal fashion will be harmful for the children. When that's the case—when experts support this decision—I recommend that my clients engage in whatever battle is necessary to get what the children need. This is one of those times when you cannot live with another outcome for the sake of your children.

Want to reveal that you're placing your own needs ahead of your children's needs? Count parenting days. Parents who engage in a game of "he's got the kids more than I've got the kids" or "I need sixty percent of the days in the year" are communicating loud and clear to everyone that their first concern is winning, not the children. I guarantee you, the kid's not counting days. The kid's just trying to adjust to being shunted back and forth. Don't keep a scorecard.

Other times, that's not the case at all. Other times, what's best for the kids is that both parents bend over backwards to make sure their children come through the divorce with good feelings about and good access to both parents.

Let's say that again: *What you most likely need to do is bend over backwards to make sure your children come through the divorce with good feelings about and good access to both parents.*

The first step in placing your kids first is to separate your feelings of loss from what's best for kids. One of the most difficult aspects of a divorce for many parents is that they can't imagine their lives without seeing their children every day—even if they want their children to have a good relationship and spend time with their STBX. So if you're a parent going through a divorce, you must be prepared to deal with your feelings of loss, not just of your spouse, but of your relationship with your children as it exists today.

When you start to manipulate things because of your own feelings of loss, that's when you mess things up.

THE GIFT OF CO-PARENTING

Who's the gatekeeper for your children? You know, the one who sets up doctor appointments, signs them up for activities, gets them to play dates or soccer practice. The one who knows when the next school project is due and what the car pool rotation is.

Even in an age of two-income families, one person typically ends up being the primary, if not the sole, gatekeeper for the children. Traditionally the mother has been the gatekeeper, and I still see that most often. Dad may still be the one who takes on these child duties less because his job is to go to work and earn the biggest chunk of the family income. But the opposite is becoming prevalent.

Drawing Enemy Lines

"He dropped the kids off with his parents for five hours while he played golf on his parenting day! I can't believe he did that!"

Get a grip. Those aren't just "his parents" who spent five hours of your STBX's parenting time with the kids. Like it or not, those two people are your children's grandparents. And like it or not, you do not want to deprive your children of a wonderful and memorable relationship with their grandparents. Trust me, you do not.

You may hate his parents. His parents may hate you. You may be ready and eager to draw enemy lines among extended family. But your STBX's parents and siblings and nieces and nephews are your children's grandparents and aunts and uncles and cousins. Your children are still related by blood even if you're no longer related by marriage. Don't compound the potential trauma of divorce by trying to force your children to divorce half their extended family.

Additional caveat: Turnabout can seem like fair play. If you try to interfere with your children's relationship with your STBX's family, your STBX can attempt to do the same. Is that really what you want? Set the precedent that's right for your children.

In a divorce, the person who is accustomed to seeing the kids every day and managing their lives—the gatekeeper—can feel as if the STBX is invading personal territory when a request is made for a more active role in the children's lives. A lot of conflict can arise when the parent who never set foot in the pediatrician's office now wants to show up, ask questions, offer an opinion. Gatekeepers may feel they are losing their jobs, along with their spouses, homes or communities.

Being able to accept this changing gatekeeper role as a natural occurrence is a plus for the children and the gatekeeping parent.

If you make a healthy adjustment to this new day when you're not the only parent taking an active role in your children's lives, you will find a great deal of liberation. Having been a single parent for many years, I should have been so lucky as to have an ex-husband who wanted to go to the doctor appointments or be part of the car pool rotation. Most of my clients who have traditionally been the gatekeepers have learned to appreciate the freedom of not being with kids all the time. Everybody needs a break from the grind of 24/7 single-parenting.

Accept co-parenting not as something being taken away from you, but as a gift that can make your life simpler and fuller—and your child's life richer.

Successful co-parenting occurs when both parents learn to treat their exes not as former spouses whose presence in life needs to be minimized, but as their partners in raising the children they created together. That should be a no-brainer. But we all know it isn't. *Children become the victims during divorce because parents aren't mature enough to continue to be co-parents once they're no longer spouses.*

So a father pretends he's the only parent and signs up a son or daughter for soccer without telling the mother, despite the fact that the soccer schedule will inevitably impact the mother's life as well. Mom doesn't put down dad as an emergency contact, so nobody calls dad when a son or daughter falls at school and breaks an arm. Project deadlines get missed because parents can't agree on who's going to help their child complete the project. Grades suffer because parents argue about who's supposed to buy supplies or help with homework, or simply don't communicate sufficiently about school.

One of the best things divorcing parents can do is set aside their own egos and really evaluate who is best suited to assume certain roles in their kid's life and at what times. We all have different skill sets and schedules; children are the winners when the grown-ups in their lives can acknowledge who is best suited to supporting them in certain ways and who is not. Who is best at getting school projects finished on time? Whose schedule allows for the most reliable transportation to soccer games? Can both parents be cooperative enough to share doctor duty?

It's not about which parent wants it most or which one has been wronged and deserves it most. It's about what arrangements serve the children's needs best.

SHOW KIDS YOU'RE STILL A FAMILY

One of the important things for you to understand is that most kids want their parents to get back together. Kids are raised on fairy tales and fantasy, right? So why should we be surprised to learn that, even after a divorce is final, children may harbor a secret, happily-ever-after fantasy that the family will be restored?

You don't want to mislead or confuse your children, of course. You should be very clear that there will be a divorce and that mommy and daddy will not be staying married or living together any more.

Even so, why would you not want to give your children the next best thing by showing up for all the events that signal "family" to your children? Why wouldn't you want to create the kind of Wiser Divorce that allows you and your ex to jointly attend school events, birthday parties, graduations, maybe even some holidays? If you want to give your children their fantasy family, and the closest you can get is to be friendly and let your kids know their parents don't hate each other, why would you not make every effort to give them this very significant gift?

Getting there over the long haul starts with how you conduct yourself during the early stages of the divorce process. How you handle these conflicts now is likely to become the ingrained pattern of parenting in the future. For your children's sake, commit to getting it right.

When it comes to your children, make up your mind not to try to win an argument, but to win an agreement.

Remember the idea of envisioning different rooms during the divorce process? One room where civilized negotiation and healthy communication take place. Another room where you take your emotions. Let's build another room. Start to carve out a small space where you and your ex-partner agree to love and support your children, together.

Children often become extremely protective of their parents, sometimes especially so if one parent seems more vulnerable or more like a victim than the other parent during a divorce. Watch for signs of this and pay attention to your own communication to make sure you aren't contributing to this heavy burden of responsibility your child is carrying. When you devalue the other parent, you're devaluing your child.

TAILOR-MADE CO-PARENTING

Back to parenting time and co-parenting.

If you're truly going to be making decisions based on what's best for your kids, it's important to seek out and accept the advice of people who know more about child development and the psychology of children and divorce than you do. If you have chosen to participate in a collaborative divorce (a model covered in Chapter Two), you'll receive the tremendous benefit of having a child specialist available to you as part of your collaborative team.

These professionals can be available to you, however, in any type of divorce. Don't resist what they're telling you. Yes, in many ways you know your kids better than they do. They, however, know things you can't possibly know yet—things like how your child will be impacted by divorce in the future. They've been there. Listen to them.

Many parents are surprised to learn that one child in the family may not require or flourish under the same custody or scheduling arrangements as other children in the family. The reason for this may have to do with the particular developmental needs of your children—children with autism, for example, tend to cope better when they have an extremely consistent schedule—as well as the age differences and personalities of your children.

The child specialist in your case can help you understand your children's developmental stages and how those differences should be taken into account when developing custody or co-parenting schedules.

A 17-year-old, for example, can spend a week at mom's and a week at dad's without experiencing it as traumatic. Of course, that's partly because a 17-year-old won't be spending as much time with parents anyway. But it's more than that. A 17-year-old has a better grasp of how quickly a week passes, how short a time seven days really is.

Younger children have less ability to grasp the concept of time. For a 6-year-old, a week may feel like a really long time to be away from the person who has been the primary parent, the one who has always prepared their food and given them a bath and tucked them into bed and driven them to school. For a young child, a co-parenting schedule of alternating weeks may not work. A week is too long. They miss the other parent too

◇◇

Things Change

Christmas was a very big deal for Lynda. A very big deal.

When Lynda and Randy decided to divorce, their children were pre-teens. For a dozen Christmas seasons, the holidays had followed a picture-perfect pattern for Lynda, Randy and their two girls.

Christmas Eve always looked the same. Lynda cooked, and all the aunts and uncles and cousins came over to decorate Christmas cookies. At dusk on Christmas Eve, everyone piled in the car to head for the Christmas Eve church service. For Lynda, the ritual of Christmas Eve mattered more than any other family ritual.

Randy, of course, had the same tradition of spending Christmas Eve with his two girls. And he expected to continue to share in their lives on this special day of anticipation and excitement. Can you do the cookie decorating party one day early sometimes, he asked his ex, so I can make some new traditions with the girls?

It seemed reasonable to Randy and totally unreasonable to Lynda, who felt her entire holiday would be ruined if she had to change a single detail of the traditions she had built with her girls. Besides, Randy wasn't even Christian. So what did Christmas Eve even mean to him?

They couldn't reach a compromise, so they went before a judge. The court determined they would have alternating holidays; all holidays, including Christmas Eve.

WISING UP: Just because things can't be the way they were, doesn't mean they can't be great again. The question for you to answer is how much time do you want to spend agonizing about the fact that things will never be exactly the same again? And are you really agonizing on behalf of your children or is this really about you? Even if it's both, your children will adjust and you will help them do that!

much during these seven days. Even though they may seem to grasp that they will see the other parent at some point, the concept of a week is too hard for them to process.

The issue of not seeing either parent for days or a week in a row can be even more traumatic for a toddler. This can feel like the end of life as a toddler knows it. Their language and reasoning skills just don't allow toddlers to understand explanations about what's going on.

What about babies? Enlightened courts don't automatically impose equal parenting schedule times for infants, with long absences from one parent or the other. There's a good reason for that. Developmental psychology tells us that babies form emotional attachments through frequent and consistent contact. If the contact is disrupted by long periods without one parent or another, babies may not bond well to that parent. So the best way

When Danger Lurks

Wanting to be a good co-parent doesn't mean ignoring possible danger for your child at the other parent's home.

Travis and Sheila had one young son when they divorced, and they agreed to an equal parenting time schedule. Sheila started dating someone Travis sensed was unsavory, and when Sheila's boyfriend moved in with her, Travis did a background check. Sheila's new live-in had been in prison for many years for armed robbery of a bank. Not to mention he had multiple drunk driving convictions since he was released.

Travis, rightfully, took legal action to ban Sheila from having their son when the boyfriend was present. After a hearing, the judge agreed the ban was best for their son. Sheila was so infatuated and controlled by the new boyfriend that she quit seeing her son rather than tell her boyfriend to leave during her parenting time.

Tragically, Sheila died in a bizarre accident while on vacation with her boyfriend, who was later convicted for her murder.

WISING UP: Sometimes you absolutely must protect your children from the other parent's choices.

for babies to form an emotional attachment is for both parents to have frequent interaction with and caretaking of a baby. That's how a bond is formed at that life stage.

What's important is to understand your particular child's developmental needs, given their ages, their personalities, and their caregiver histories. And if you want healthy children who grow into healthy, well-adjusted adults, you want your kids to be bonded with both their parents. The ones who don't can be the ones who have a hard time forming healthy bonds as adults, as well.

GETTING GOOGLY-EYED

Speaking of bonding, some divorcing parents just can't wait for their children to bond with the new love of their life.

People are idiots about this. One of the most popular ways divorcing parents demonstrate that their children don't really come first is when they are indulging in a new relationship, either during the divorce or after the divorce is final, and they let their children know about it. They fall in love, get all googly-eyed again, and don't understand how profoundly this will impact their kids.

Just because you've finished mourning the loss of your marriage doesn't mean your children have finished mourning the loss of their family.

You should not even think of introducing a child to someone new until long after your divorce; most experts say wait at least six months to a year. Major life events for children—and a new love relationship for a divorced parent is certainly a major life event—affect them. You may think you've found the love of your life, but in reality you may just be experiencing the first in a series of serial attachments that come along post-divorce.

Even if you have found the love of your life, it is not the love of your children's lives.

Believe it or not, some parents will introduce a new person to their children when they're only sleeping with them. Why in the world would mature, rational parents introduce a child to someone they're only sleeping with? The answer: They wouldn't.

Unless you are planning to marry this person, soon, don't even think about introducing your new love to your children. And quite honestly, if you are just getting divorced, you shouldn't be thinking of marrying anyone yet.

Remember, the number one criteria for making decisions is what's best for your children. It's not about how badly you want your new love to see what adorable children you had a hand in producing. It's certainly not about wanting your children to see what an amazing stepparent you're lining up for them. It's not about your own desire to fill the void in your own life by recreating a fantasy family for weekends at the lake or popcorn and movies on Friday nights. It's not about what you want. It's about what's best for your children.

By the way, many children feel unappreciated and unloved when your time with them after the divorce always includes your new love. What they really want to experience is your devoted attention to them and them alone as they navigate their own feelings about their parents' marriage ending. They need to know they've not been displaced, and that they still come first.

Remember, your child is going through a divorce, too.

◇◇

Playing One-Up

This is a doozy from my own life. When my daughter was five, I confided in my ex that I was buying her first real bicycle for Christmas. This was no easy feat— I was broke and saved for months to get her this gift.

It was his year to have Christmas, so I intended to tell her when she returned that Santa had left this gift for her while she was at her father's house. She called me excitedly on Christmas Day to tell me about her new bike her father had bought her.

WISING UP: Trying to one-up your ex with your kids is not the definition of co-parenting.

Another break-up with someone you've brought into their lives could stir up all the confusion, the pain, and the uncertainty for a child who may barely be healing from the previous confusion, pain and uncertainty. And rebound relationships are notoriously hard to sustain.

Don't do this to your children.

Whatever your motive, don't go there just because you're having a great time being in a new relationship.

GROUND RULES FOR TELLING THE KIDS

Communication sets the tone for a divorce. At no other point in the process is healthy communication more critical than it is when it comes to how you talk to your children about divorce.

> If you want to be a loving parent to your children, act like the divorce is not devastating you and will have a good outcome for everyone. Remember, the more you act it, the more you are it.

How you and your STBX talk to your children about your divorce will have a profound impact on how they receive the information, how they react to it and how they heal from it. And they will need to heal, even though they can be just as happy and well-adjusted growing up in two households as they would have been growing up in one—sometimes even more so if they no longer have to experience conflict and unhappy parents and a bad role model for marriage. Divorce can wound and scar children as surely as it can wound and scar adults. We can tell ourselves all day long that children are resilient—and they are—but how we communicate can determine just how resilient they are.

When it's time to talk to the children about the inevitability of divorce, here are the basic ground rules:

- Mom and dad tell them together.

- The scorned or betrayed parent does not run to the kids and spill the beans.

- Neither parent blames the other parent for anything.

- Don't cry. Your kids don't need to see you fall apart.

- Shield them from the business of divorce.

- Show up when they need you. Together.

- Reassure them of your love.

- Get coaching in co-parenting and healthy communication.

- Take your children to a counselor, even if you don't think your children are traumatized. Providing them with a safe, neutral third party to confide in can go far in helping them positively respond to this transition.

What do your children need to hear from you? They need to hear that their lives will be minimally disrupted. They need to hear that they will be going to the same school, engaging in the same activities, will have a degree of stability. They need to hear that you are going to come up with a good plan for continuing to be a family for them, even if it will be a divorced family.

Of course, you can't tell them these things if they aren't true. So you owe it to your children to make these things true to the greatest possible degree. If you do that, you'll be amazed how much it will accelerate your own healing as well.

What your children don't need to hear is all the details. Or how you personally feel about your STBX at this moment. Remember, this is your child's other parent. They may not feel about your STBX the way you feel. In fact, they probably shouldn't. Children stay healthier when they can continue to love and respect and admire both their parents. The things you say about their other parent, and how you say them, will be a major factor in whether they come away from the divorce with positive feelings about both parents or negative feelings that can take a lifetime to heal.

I feel so strongly about this that I've fired clients who say too much to their children about divorce.

I remember one woman who told me, as many people do, that her children were her "number one priority" in her divorce. She clearly did not know what that meant. When her STBX's attorney kept asking why the children knew about every court date and what information was in court pleadings, my client responded, "My children are entitled to know everything."

No, they weren't. Her children were still in grade school. They were entitled to parents with healthy boundaries and a commitment to doing what was best for them, not the details that helped their mother justify her own anger or bitterness in the moment.

Remember, divorcing is your decision, not your kids' decision. Focus as much of your energy as possible on protecting your children from the emotional fall-out of this experience. Your number one parenting job during a divorce is to work with your STBX to make things work out best for the kids. It's about helping your children grieve. It's about making your children whole no matter what that looks like and no matter what you have to do to make it happen.

That's how you create positive solutions, even for your kids.

8 Choose the Right Attorney

Forget everything Hollywood has ever taught you about attorneys.

Movies and TV perpetuate myths about attorneys. On screen, we are either saints or sleaze. Either we fight for justice against all odds and rescue our clients from all manner of evil, or we are cutthroat liars and cheats.

Here's what you really want in an attorney: a strategic ally who will tell you the truth, even if it's a truth you don't want to hear, and who will guide you to the best and most realistic outcome for you based on your particular circumstances.

Your attorney is not your mother or your best friend or your therapist.

Your attorney is not your STBX's worst enemy.

Good attorneys are teachers, guides, experts in their field who can give you the best- and worst-case scenarios on issues, so you understand your choices and the likely outcomes.

If your finances permit, hiring an attorney is one of your first steps once it's clear that divorce is in your future. It's a decision that is going to impact the cost of your divorce, the emotional tone of your divorce, the future of your children, and your own likelihood of moving forward into your Best New Life.

The decision of who will make this legal journey with you is one of the most important decisions you'll make during the process. So don't just do a search online and pick someone whose office is convenient or look at the ads in one of the free phone directories that land on your porch a couple of times a year. Don't hire your college roommate's daughter who is just out of law school and needs the work. Don't hire the guy from your Monday morning networking group who specializes in real estate law but is a really nice guy and someone you are positive will take good care of you.

Do your homework.

If your relationship with your STBX is healthy enough, you can both commit to finding attorneys who will help you achieve a good divorce. It starts with finding two attorneys with the common goal of helping both of you walk away with your dignity intact and the future of your children as a primary concern. Two attorneys who will work with you to minimize the economic impact to the family.

SOMEONE YOU CAN TRUST

Finding an attorney starts with *finding the right attorney for you.*

A lot of people choose their attorneys because a friend had a great attorney who a) kicked their STBX's butt; b) made them rich in the settlement; c) provided life-saving emotional support; or d) all of the above. Maybe that same attorney will be perfect for you, too. Or maybe you have different goals, a different personality, different support needs, a different perspective on what it means to achieve a successful divorce.

You need to find the attorney who is *right for you*, not the attorney who was right for your best friend or your cousin's co-worker. Take recommendations, but plan to interview several attorneys. Different attorneys have distinctly different client interaction methods as well as different approaches to the process of divorce. Your attorney's level of expertise (which sometimes means vast differences in hourly rates) should be what is necessary for your particular case. You don't need one of the highest priced attorneys in town if you have few assets and no children. But you very well may need that attorney if you have complex financial issues or know there are a lot of fights to come.

Another part of the personality equation to pay attention to in hiring an attorney is how that attorney thinks about, talks about, or talks to your STBX and the attorney for the other side.

◇◇

What a Good Attorney Will Do

When you are interviewing an attorney, ask them if and how they do these things:

- Identify reasonable goals to achieve.

- Outline how to achieve your goals and explain the cost of achieving them.

- Help guide you or mentor you through the divorce.

- Provide honest advice even if it's not what you want to hear or don't think is fair.

- Advise you of the law.

- Discuss ways to resolve your case, including looking outside the box for creative solutions that the law might not offer you.

- Use honey as effectively as aggressive advocacy, and understand when each is needed.

- Use phone calls and meetings when appropriate instead of handling every single thing in writing.

- Hold in-person meetings with both attorneys and spouses early and often as needed.

Some people want a bulldog attorney who will go on the attack against the other side. While you certainly want someone who can and will stand up for you, an attack-dog attorney can work against you by unnecessarily elevating the adversarial atmosphere and quashing the cooperative attitude that usually works in favor of win-win compromises.

This is not to say that your attorney shouldn't be a zealous advocate. But there's a line that can be crossed between strong advocate and attack-dog representation. And you can spot it easily: You will see personal attacks against your STBX versus an assertion of why you are correct or why things should happen a certain way. If your attorney calls the other attorney names, if

Top 10 Signs You Have the Wrong Attorney

Chances are you have the wrong attorney if your attorney:

1. Doesn't promptly return your calls or emails.

2. Doesn't help you set reasonable goals and discuss strategies for achieving goals.

3. Fights with the other side in ways that are more personal, less professional.

4. Encourages you to slam your STBX.

5. Doesn't prepare you in advance for hearings or mediation or interaction with experts.

6. Doesn't regularly provide you with a bill of itemized services.

7. Doesn't try to settle your case without litigation or otherwise look for the most expeditious and economical ways to get you divorced, even if it means agreeing to something other than what they think "the court" would do.

8. Gets caught being dishonest or is willing to cover up your lies, including misrepresentations, to the court.

9. Can't admit he or she made a mistake.

10. Makes you feel uncomfortable, denigrates you, ignores you, or make advances toward you.

your attorney is disrespectful or makes it personal, that's a lot different from being assertive and vigorous in arguing a point.

You want an attorney who can be aggressive when it's needed instead of someone who can *only* be aggressive; the best attorneys can modify their responses based on what's needed under the particular circumstances of your divorce.

And there's always a difference between being professionally aggressive and launching personal attacks.

One of the most important traits to look for in an attorney is someone who will be honest with you, even if it's something you don't want to hear. You never want an attorney who will only tell you what you want to hear—too much is at stake to engage with an attorney who doesn't have the gumption to tell you the truth. This includes everything from being honest with you about the importance of breaking what may be your old patterns of fighting with your STBX, to arguing about minutia, to continuing a tone of voice that becomes part of the soundtrack for a bitter divorce and a bitter divorced family.

LISTEN TO YOUR ATTORNEY

Look for the attorney who can empathize with the circumstances that brought you here without encouraging you to keep repeating them. Your attorney will be standing up for you in a legal engagement. If he can't stand up to you, how effective will he or she be standing up for you in front of other attorneys, in front of judges? No, you need an independent person who will tell you what you may not want to hear. Of course it is up to you to decide if you will listen or not; if you don't, it could well be to your detriment.

Look for someone you're comfortable with, but remember that your attorney is a strategic advisor, not a best-friend candidate. Your attorney must educate you, mentor you, advise you, help you set goals, help you to resolve your case without litigation, but fight for you in court if necessary. Your attorney must be sensitive to your specific goals and challenges and understand what you need to get through your divorce.

And look for someone you trust. Period. There is no "but" after that one. You never, never want an attorney at your side that you cannot trust absolutely. This is a strategic relationship, and your attorney is a strategic partner who will shape your future. Look for someone you trust.

ASK THE RIGHT QUESTIONS

When hiring an attorney, you need to express your goals for your divorce. Unfortunately, in those first early, confusing days, you may not be clear about your goals. Or you might not have realistic goals. Having this discussion with a prospective attorney is a very good way to get to know how the attorney across the conference table views divorce. If he or she is asking you questions that you're not clear how to answer, turn the questions back on the attorney.

Here are a few of the questions you may want to ask the attorney during the interview:

- How will I know which of my goals are realistic?

- What questions should I be asking myself as I begin the process of divorce?

- What information do we need to settle my case and answer my questions and how will we get it?

- What particular expertise will you offer for negotiating a settlement?

- What is the expected timeline for my divorce?

- Do you think we'll need to hire outside experts? How much will that cost?

- Who from your firm will be working on my case? (Some firms have lower-cost associates or paralegals who will be sharing in the work, which will be cost-effective for you. Or your case may require multiple partners working on it at the same time because of its complexity.)

- How does the firm bill? How often?

- What is the best way for us to communicate?

- How will you keep me up-to-date about everything that happens in my case?

If you have an attorney who is caught up in the war of a courtroom battle, hooked on banging the drums, that attorney can't place your interests first.

Try to get yourself into that emotion-free zone so you can listen carefully to how the attorney is responding to your questions. Do the procedures that are being described make sense to you? Make notes you can refer to later, when you may be in a better state of mind to evaluate what's been said. If you don't understand what's being said, interrupt and ask for clarification.

One clue: If the attorney you're interviewing makes you feel

Top Three Things You Can Do to Create a Divorce that Works for You:

- Listen to and trust your attorney
- Be an honest and trustworthy client
- Follow your attorney's advice

too uncomfortable to ask questions, it's probably the wrong attorney.

Another clue: If the attorney you're interviewing is impatient or makes you feel dumb about the questions you do ask, it's probably the wrong attorney.

And one more clue: If the attorney you're interviewing tries to intimidate you by implying that bad things will happen if you go with a different attorney, it's probably the wrong attorney.

A final clue: If the attorney you're interviewing implies that they'll be doing you a favor by taking on your case, it's probably the wrong attorney.

Listen to your gut reactions about this person. Compare your gut reaction to each of the attorneys you've interviewed. You're about to make a decision that's going to impact your future—a decision that will take money out of your pocket and put it into this firm's pocket. *You* are hiring *them.*

After your initial one-on-one consultation, you should feel a sense of relief, not a sense of trepidation. You should walk away with a sense that someone is going to have your back as you maneuver through this foreign, and sometimes dangerous, territory called divorce.

TALKING MONEY

Never be afraid to talk money with your attorney. Always remember that when you settle on a strategy for your divorce, you are making decisions about how much this divorce is going to cost. Some strategies can be accomplished more quickly and easily than others. Some take more time and money. And the longer your divorce takes, the more money it will cost you.

When you hire an attorney, you're not paying for results; you're buying time. This is a very important concept to grasp and remember. It could take many, many hours of your attorney's time before you can get to a result. Or you may ask your attorney to do things that never result in a tangible result. Talk to your attorney about various strategies and the timeframe for every scenario. That will allow you to make an informed decision about the priorities you want to pursue.

You will be billed for everything your attorney does that takes time. Reading your emails? Takes time. Tracking down the nitty-gritty details about your STBX's presumed infidelity? Time. Complaining about the fact your STBX brought the kids home a half hour late? Time. And time is money.

A good attorney will try to resolve issues by searching for maneuvers that will enable everyone to get what they want. An attorney who is focused on keeping your STBX from getting his or her needs met is not going to help you achieve a good divorce.

It isn't that you shouldn't communicate with your attorney. It's that you want clarity from your attorney about the most efficient way to communicate certain information. Maybe it's via email in which you list all the questions that have occurred to you over the last week. Maybe it's face-to-face. Maybe you just need a quick phone call.

It isn't that you don't want your attorney to do a thorough job of fact-finding, either. It's that you want to be on the search for the most pertinent facts. Determining the market value of a family business, for example, will be time and money well-spent. Determining what hotels your STBX went to and how often during a fling may be little more than fuel for your outrage and increase the fees you pay.

Any money you spend on attorney fees ideally should be closely connected to achieving your strategic goals.

One cost you can't control is attorneys' fees spent because of how your STBX's attorney practices law. Your attorney must review everything the other attorney sends or files, must return their phone calls, and must respond as needed. If the other attorney is a good professional, these costs will just be the usual costs necessary to facilitate your divorce. If the other attorney is the war-monger type, these costs may dramatically increase the costs of your divorce. You can't control your fees in such situations, but you can find out from your attorney the options in your jurisdiction for receiving a reimbursement fee award.

EXPENSIVE HAND-HOLDING

Often we're so vulnerable when we come to our first attorney interview that we think we want an attorney who will be a best friend, a confidante, a protector, and a counselor. This is an understandable impulse, but one I suggest you be careful about continuing to follow as your divorce unfolds.

An attorney who will fill all those roles for you is likely to be more expensive simply because he or she is going to have to spend additional time hand-holding, comforting, and propping

◇◇

Yep, Your Attorney Might Do This, But It's Gonna Be Expensive:

- Be your counselor.

- Explain how your friend' or family member's divorce is different from yours.

- Interact with your mom, dad, sister, etc., who want to come to all your meetings and either insert their two-cents' worth or have everything explained to their satisfaction.

- Try to get you answers to matters not relevant to your case.

Yep, he or she can do all those things. But they're sand through the hour glass. And that's going to show up on your bill.

you up emotionally. To some extent that may be and should be what your attorney needs to do for you. Maybe they don't mind at all—the more you talk the more they make. But if every email, meeting or phone call involves hand-holding or just listening to you ramble, you are doubling the expense of your divorce.

A good attorney will be empathetic but will try to redirect you if you are wasting good money purely on venting. If they don't, it can be an indication of an attorney who will approach your case emotionally instead of strategically.

Attorneys themselves learn this as their years of practice unfold. In my early cases, it was hard to get to that emotion-free zone with my clients. In my earliest years of practice I wanted to help them in any way I could. I wanted to be their savior. Their problems were my problems. I would do anything my clients wanted or seemed to need. I woke up thinking about their cases. I became enmeshed with my clients. Their fight was mine, too.

One of my first clients was an alcoholic who couldn't function in life. A lot of money was at stake. I let her call me at home. I became her caretaker. To make sure she arrived where she was supposed to be sober and on time, I would pick her up and drive her to depositions and court appearances. She once left a box in my car that turned out to contain marijuana.

I thought I was helping, and maybe to some extent I did save her from her worst self. In the end, I enabled her to get to the other side of her divorce without really preparing for her new life. Divorce could have been part of her process of hitting bottom, preparing her for her Next Best Life. Instead, when it was all over, she was still an alcoholic who couldn't function.

I was a basket case from juggling her case and her life.

You want an attorney who can get to the strategic and emotion-free zone. Some attorneys never get there even after years of practice. Every case still becomes their call to arms for battle, and there is no truth but their client's truth.

Those are not the attorneys for you.

NO MAGIC WANDS

Hiring an attorney to help you divorce successfully is a lot like choosing a doctor if you have cancer or some other life-altering illness.

Maybe you're the kind of person who's comfortable going to the doctor, describing your symptoms, and nodding when the doctor says, "Okay, here's the diagnosis. Here's your pill. Come back in six weeks."

Or maybe you'd rather find the doctor who will make you a partner in your treatment, the kind of doctor who'll say, "This is how I've made the diagnosis. Here are treatment options. This is the option I recommend. Here's the outcome you can expect from your treatment."

If you're one of those people who go to the doctor, take whatever pills are prescribed and never ask any questions, never get a second opinion and place all your trust in whatever the physician tells you, you may bring that same mindset to working with your divorce attorney. You may think attorneys have all the answers, and you can now bury your head in the sand until it's over. I've seen a lot of people who hire an attorney and say, in effect, "Here is my box of junk. Please take your magic wand and sprinkle your fairy dust and make everything right again."

If that's your mindset, change it right now. I don't want you looking for the attorney who will say, "OK, dear, everything is going to be fine. Let me take care of this for you."

Studies show that patients who are actively involved in their healing journey have the best outcome. The same is true for people who are getting divorced. Once you've hired an attorney, you still have a role. Your attorney doesn't have a magic wand. Your attorney is your partner.

Approach the process of identifying, interviewing and hiring an attorney with a realistic expectation of what a good attorney

◇◇

Yes, You CAN Change Attorneys

You might initially hire an attorney you feel is the one to help you through divorce. But if after working with this attorney you feel uninformed, frustrated, scared, or just uncomfortable, you should not be shy about changing counsel.

Rob had consulted with me from time to time after his divorce. His ex was receiving spousal maintenance from him every month, but she was living with her new boyfriend, who was now contributing substantially to her monthly financial needs. This meant Rob's monthly payments should be reduced or eliminated. When the time to act came, however, there was going to be a three-week wait to see me and he went with another attorney.

From the start, Rob felt uncomfortable about his interactions with the new attorney. A telling example of the small things that began to add up was the new attorney's reaction when Rob brought in a file on his communications with his ex. Rob is a very detailed person; the file was comprehensive, a stack of papers four inches high.

The new attorney told Rob, "Don't worry about that right now. I'll look through those if we go to trial."

Rob knew from earlier conversations with me that those communications might hold the key to a successful strategy for securing his desired outcome—and could, in fact, help us avoid a trial and the expenses associated with going to court.

When Rob asked what their strategy would be, the new attorney said, "Let's see how the case progresses and then set a strategy."

Rob wasn't comfortable with going into the process with no strategy and ultimately moved the case to me. I read everything he brought to me, and we discussed the appropriate strategy for his case.

In Rob's situation, the reasons to back away from his attorney were subtle. Other times, the reasons aren't subtle at all. And in some cases, people ignore the signs until the problems become a crisis.

Another client, who came to me after firing her first attorney, reported that after a long session of mediation, her attorney left the conference room with the other attorney. When he returned, he reported to her, "This is what we've agreed to."

When she declined, her STBX-attorney started screaming, "This is my reputation at stake! You *will* settle for this!"

In another case, one that was long, protracted, and involved high dollars, the client came to me for a "second opinion." She described to me significant abuse that occurred during the marriage, which her current attorney was brushing under the rug.

She asked me if I believed her. Having worked with many battered women, I found her credible and I did believe her. I told her so. She started to cry and told me I was the first attorney to acknowledge her story and express belief about what she was saying. I took her case, and while the abuse did not impact the outcome of her case, her trust in me did.

Or take the case of Claire. She came to us with boxes of information she had given her first attorney, who had never looked at it. She didn't have any understanding of the family's finances, because her STBX always handled the finances during their long marriage. All she wanted to do was understand her circumstances, and her attorney wasn't answering her questions.

We took the case, we were able to educate her on her finances, and she was then able to make educated settlement decisions.

Many of the serious misfires attorneys make are rooted in their desire to win, or to just make life easier on themselves. One woman who came to me for help in undoing a settlement deal told me her mediation had gone on for twelve hours with no progress. Yet her former attorney had pressured her to take the deal that was being offered, despite the fact she was sobbing uncontrollably and had many unanswered questions.

When she finally announced, between sobs, that she was leaving, her attorney followed her, screaming at her, "You are going to stay! You are going to get this done!"

He bullied her into accepting the deal, despite the fact that he knew she was on anti-depressants to cope with her emotions over the divorce.

As she left, she heard him saying to the other attorney that he was glad they had settled because he needed to prepare for another trial.

When she came to me, we were able to undo the deal. But it cost her a lot.

can—and should—do for you. Your attorney's number one priority is to help you identify and understand what issues need to be settled, either through mediation or negotiation or at trial, identify what information is needed and what questions need to be answered, and, once all the facts are known, predict likely outcomes—the wins and no-wins.

WHAT HAPPENS NEXT

Choosing your attorney carefully and with intentionality is vitally important because of what comes next. Having just told you to be an active participant with your attorney, what comes next may seem counter-intuitive, even contradictory. It's vital—*if* you have the right attorney:

Do what your attorney tells you to do.

Once you've decided on an attorney ... once you and your attorney, together, have identified the issues to be settled ... once the information has been gathered ... once goals have been named and strategies agreed upon, together ... you have one major role to play. And that is to listen carefully to your attorney and follow his or her recommendations.

To go back to the comparison with a doctor-patient relationship, you improve your chances of a good outcome when you choose your doctor carefully and select a mutually-agreed-upon treatment plan, then actively participate while following your doctor's advice about that plan. If you start chemotherapy, but only show up for every other treatment because your best friend recommended a new form of therapy, you may not have the best outcome. If you agree to surgery, you aren't well-served if you don't follow the pre-op and post-op instructions.

The same thing is true in a divorce. The same principle applies once you've found the right attorney, the attorney you trust and have partnered with to build a strategy based on the outcomes you want. If you don't trust your attorney enough to follow his or her advice—even if you don't always agree with it—you either have the wrong attorney or the wrong attitude about your divorce.

Don't take another step until you've evaluated whether you truly have the wrong attorney or whether you're allowing fear or stubbornness or well-meaning friends or family to call the shots for you.

Listen to your attorney. Follow the plan you've agreed to. A good attorney has been down this road before, knows which

---

An Attorney's Pet Peeves

When you're taking self-destructive actions, you're making it very difficult for an attorney to help you achieve your goals. Attorneys hate knowing you're sabotaging yourself. So here is what's on our (OK, my) list of pet peeves about clients.

- Clients who hire me but don't take my advice.

- Clients who can't get to the big picture.

- Clients who misrepresent the facts, sometimes known as lying.

- Clients who take significant actions in the middle of divorce without discussing it first– things like buying a house, selling a car, taking the children to a psychiatrist. Anything

that might be pertinent to your divorce should be discussed with your attorney first. When in doubt, ask.

- Clients who believe I have a vial of fairy dust I can sprinkle to make everything OK.

- Clients whose negativity is the only emotion they bring to their divorce.

- Clients who want revenge. There's an ancient Chinese proverb that applies here: When you seek revenge, dig two graves.

The last thing you want to be is "that" client, the one who frustrates and exhausts your attorney, who sucks every bit of energy out of him or her. The one attorneys groan about when your call comes in. You are not helping your attorney help you when these are your actions.

hairpin curves to avoid and where all the potholes are. You disregard a good attorney's advice at your own peril.

Good clients listen to their attorneys and follow their advice.

WHAT GOOD CLIENTS DO

Part two of hiring a good attorney, then, is being a good client.

Good clients listen to their attorneys about which outcomes are realistic and which are not and do not look for unrealistic outcomes in a divorce settlement.

Good clients realize they aren't victims, but had a hand in creating this divorce.

Good clients are clear about their goals and remember to tell their attorney if those goals change.

Good clients, however, don't change their goals frequently and on a whim.

Good clients tell their attorneys the truth because the best attorney in the world can't always help them effectively if a lie comes back to bite them on the rear end.

Good clients bring their best self to the table, leaving negativity and old relationship patterns at the door.

Good clients read everything they receive from their attorneys—including their bills. This helps them maintain a realistic sense of what's going on. I've had clients who don't read their bills because they think it will help them stay in an emotion-free zone. Maybe they want to remain in denial about what is really going on. Then, when they do open the bills, they don't understand what the charges reflect.

Good clients know the sand (money) is running through the hour glass and that their actions impact how quickly the sand runs out. A good client will realize quickly, for example, that the 150 emails she sent me last month just cost her an extra $10,000 because I had to take the time to wade through every one of them, decide which ones were pertinent and which ones were a waste of time, and respond appropriately. One of my clients who tended to over-communicate realized quickly that her monthly bills had tripled over a period of three months. When she finally opened her bills and she realized how much her daily emails were costing her, her need to communicate about every little detail vanished and she became much more focused and strategic in her communications.

Your Good Client Checklist

1. Read everything you get from your attorney.

2. Keep all documents related to your case organized on paper or online. Segregate your organization into headings, such as correspondence between you and your attorney, correspondence between attorneys, papers filed with the court, court orders, financial papers, and so on.

3. Read your bills line by line and notify your attorney immediately if you see an error.

4. Absent an emergency, make telephone or in-person appointments in advance when you need more than a short discussion with your attorney. This will ensure your attorney has adequate time to discuss your concerns and questions.

5. Tell your attorney if you want to review letters and court filings in advance before they are sent/filed.

6. Promptly provide your attorney with any requested information.

7. Ask your attorney the pertinent questions that will enable you to be a knowledgeable participant. This is about preparing yourself, not about the need to control everything. This is **YOUR** divorce, and you need to understand the facts, the strategy, and your options.

8. Resist the urge to tell your attorney what to do to achieve your goals. You set the goals, let your attorney set the strategy to achieve those goals.

At my firm, in addition to a standard fee agreement, we have another agreement all of our new clients sign that clearly spells out their responsibilities as clients, and our responsibilities as their attorneys. It defines what commitments we are making to them in the areas of communication, action, and goal setting, and what our expectations are in those same areas from them. That may sound simplistic. But we want our clients to understand that we can't be the best attorneys we can be unless they do their part to be healthy, cooperative clients.

The attorney-client relationship really is a partnership, but it's a new kind of partnership for most people. Figuring out how to do your part makes it work.

MANY ARROWS IN THE QUIVER

Most people who walk into my office for a first consultation still believe the end of the road leads to court.

In a sense they are right. Divorce is a legal process and ultimately the court issues the final divorce decree. The danger is in believing that all the decisions get made at that final destination.

One of the things you're looking for in an attorney is someone who can offer you many different ways to travel that road and arrive in court, if you must, with as many agreements made and facts established as possible before you get there. While you want an attorney who has achieved the art of successful trial advocacy, with the experience necessary to give you the best possible trial outcome if you must have a judge decide your case, it is also important to know what settlement method options they have used and their experience in achieving resolutions even in the worst of cases.

Does the attorney have a collaborative practice? Does this attorney engage in mediation or settlement conferences, with or without a formal mediator? Mediation or settlement conferences can occur in a number of ways. Both attorneys and their clients can meet once or have a series of meetings where options for settlement are discussed and hopefully agreed upon. Or a professional mediator can be engaged to assist in a settlement. Typically when a professional mediator is hired, the mediator is provided with a confidential memo from each side in advance, setting out the issues that need to be resolved and that side's position on settlement of each issue. The mediator's job is to broker a final agreement. Often a client and attorney sit in a different room from the other client and attorney; the mediator goes back and forth between the rooms until an agreement is reached. This is a highly effective form of settlement and allows each side to hear an objective mediator's opinion on the strengths and weaknesses of their case. You will likely also learn things about your STBX's positions and strategies you did not know before, which is not only helpful in the mediation process but will be helpful if you can't settle and must go to trial.

You should also find out if private judge or arbitration resolution methods are available in your jurisdiction. Under either method, the private judge or arbitrator is substituted for the trial judge. They will hear testimony, review exhibits, and make rulings on contested issues. Thus, you can avoid a formal court appearance, while still giving authority to a decision maker to decide the issues in your case. Many times this allows for a faster resolution of your case than you would otherwise have waiting in line for months for a court date.

What other resources does the attorney have experience with? Does this attorney recommend divorce coaches who can help you define your questions and set goals as a couple? Can this attorney recommend a communications coach? Can he or she recommend a career counselor or financial expert to help you set a realistic budget for your after-divorce life? Does this attorney frequently work with business valuators and custody evaluators?

As you look at all these factors, remember that your goal isn't to find an attorney who only handles collaborative or mediated divorces, any more than it is to find an attorney who always fights the battle in court. You certainly aren't looking for an attorney who will avoid court at all costs because that kind of attorney poses a real danger. There are attorneys who will force a settlement—even a bad settlement—just to avoid court. Court is a pain. It's a lot of work. But you must have an attorney who will go to court if it's clearly in your best interests to do so.

The goal is to find an attorney who has many arrows in his or her quiver, one who offers a multi-disciplinary approach. This is the attorney who will help you find the best solution for your circumstances.

Not all roads lead to court. But some do. You want an attorney who is confident and experienced no matter where the road leads.

9 Face the Truth About Judges and Your Day in Court

Leaving your divorce in the hands of the court system is a gamble.

Think about it: Leaving your divorce in the hands of the court translates into leaving your divorce in the hands of **one person—** the judge, whom you don't know, and who doesn't know you.

Some people think that sounds great. Judges are wise, right? Impartial. Able to cut through the crazy-making claims and accusations and dispense justice (let me translate that into non-legal terminology: *Judges will see things my way.*). Right?

Not exactly.

Judges are people, too. Which means they are unpredictable, complex, filled with biases and human foibles and blind spots.

Some of them are superbly suited to navigate and decide issues regarding the end of your marriage, and truly strive to do what's right and just. Others are irritable and cranky about having to even listen to the mess you called your marriage and the even bigger mess you call your divorce. Some of them don't like women, and some of them have issues with men. They aren't child psychologists or family counselors or experts in determining the value of your business. Some of them never even practiced family law in their pre-judge career. Most of them won't interview kids, and they certainly are unlikely to believe what you say your children say. They can't see into the dark corners of your STBX's soul and discern what a scheming, lying, trouble-making jerk you've been married to. And even if they could do all those things, they probably can't reward you or punish your STBX in the way you see fit because the law won't let them.

This is the life of a divorce judge: They go to work every day and listen to people fight, complain, and sometimes misrepresent the truth. They many times make considerably less money than the people they have to listen to fight and complain and lie. When their time in the courtroom is over, they have a mountain of paperwork waiting for them. Day after day, they read the same tedious filings and accusations and counter-accusations. Day after day, they try to make sense out of complicated, chaotic

◇◇◇

Top 10 Myths about Judges

1. Judges don't make mistakes.

2. The judge's decision is final.

3. As soon as the judge rules, all the messy wrangling is over.

4. The judge will see things your way. Or, stated another way, the judge will believe you, not your STBX.

5. The judge's ruling will vindicate your belief that your spouse was the sinner, and you were the saint.

6. Judges will hear everything you think is relevant to your marriage or divorce.

7. Your divorce will be special to the judge.

8. The judge will deliver justice as you believe "justice" to be.

9. The judge will be unbiased.

10. The judge can do what he thinks is fair, even if the law says something different. Nope, judges have to make decisions based on the law.

divorces where they are asked to play god about people's futures and decide whose "truth" is the real truth. Your divorce is just one of a multitude. No judge spends hours thinking, *That poor woman, she has been through hell!*

In fact, it's far more likely that your judge is thinking about your squabbles: *Here we go again. Two good parents saying the other is bad.* Or, *two people with more financial means than me arguing about who's going to pay for their kids' soccer uniforms.*

In other words, they aren't necessarily predisposed to be sympathetic about your circumstances or the divorce that got assigned to them (just one of hundreds or thousands on their docket).

Also remember that you don't get to pick your judge. It's the luck of the draw. Some states allow you to change a judge once without giving a reason, but then you are stuck with the next one assigned to your case, like it or not. Maybe you'll end up with someone wise and compassionate, or whose particular biases will make him or her predisposed to like your personality and your arguments better than your STBX's personality and arguments.

And maybe you won't.

Welcome to your day in court.

LOOKING FOR THE SUPREME COMMANDER OF JUSTICE

Never before have divorcing couples had so many diverse alternatives for settling their case without allowing a judge to decide their fate. Yet every day, people still throw themselves on the mercy of the court to decide their future.

Why do people do this, when there are mechanisms in place to decide their own futures?

Sometimes it is necessary because your STBX will not be reasonable in a settlement, and you have no other option or because your child's well-being is at stake. But here's what I often see: Divorcing people end up in court because of their desire to prove to the world that they are in the right.

They call it looking for justice. They say all they want is what's fair. But for most people, that translates into "I'm right, my STBX is wrong" or "I'm good, my STBX is evil."

People believe judges will see things their way because (their own) truth will prevail. You can be right all day and still have judges tell you that you're wrong. People cling to the idea that having a judge rule will equal a public punishment of their STBX and a public declaration of their own righteousness. Sometimes when people settle they have to give in, make concessions, and they tend to see going to court as the place where they will win. In the courtroom, the Supreme Commander of Justice will issue an edict clarifying good and evil for everyone.

People tell themselves there's no way in the world a court would decide in their STBX's favor—but it happens every day. Judges make rulings that seem absolutely unfathomable to the people who are on the short end of the stick in those rulings.

Every day, the courts let people down. Because that's how divorce works when we let someone else call the shots.

Judges and courts are not in the business of granting you absolution for every mistake or wrongdoing that led to your divorce. And they are not in the business of condemning, chastising or punishing the mistakes or wrongdoings of your STBX, either. Judges are there to apply the laws of your state to the dissolution of your marriage.

It's not about fairness or justice. It's about replacing one contract—the marriage contract—with another contract—the divorce contract.

But my case is different.

My STBX's behavior was so egregious ... so immoral ... so evil that any judge in the world will see how wronged I've been.

You haven't seen a divorce like this one before.

When Court Is the Only Choice

Sometimes you have no choice but to go to court. Maybe because the stakes are too high, the law is unclear, your STBX or the other attorney is unreasonable, your children's well-being is at stake, or maybe you and your STBX just have too many differences in your perceptions of reality.

Whatever the reason, you need to be prepared and prepared well. Here are some tips:

- Most jurisdictions require submission of a statement before trial outlining any agreements, contested issues, and each side's positions on the contested issues. Make sure your attorney gives you the opportunity to review this document before it goes to the judge, so you can ensure all the issues have been addressed and you are comfortable with the rulings being requested on your behalf.

- Exhibits must also usually be submitted before trial. You should trust your attorney to provide the court all the documents you'll need to rely on in presenting your case, but make sure you re-familiarize yourself with them before trial–including the exhibits your STBX will present to the court.

- Your attorney absolutely must meet with you prior to the trial to review the questions they will ask you when you are on the stand, to review with you the exhibits they will show you, and to focus you on the information they think is most important to your case. They should also instruct you on the proper demeanor for your cross-examination and discuss what topics they think may come up in your cross-examination.

- A tip about having your friends or family in the courtroom during your trial. It is usually permissible to do so, and extra support can be a good thing. But you don't need a crowd. And you certainly don't want to bring people who will gasp, make faces, or utter "liar" when your STBX is slamming you during their testimony. If they can't keep their composure, leave them at home.

Well, yes, I have. And so has the judge.

I know. I hear it all the time. Your divorce is unique. Your divorce represents such a clear-cut case of wrongdoing that the judge will immediately want to right all wrongs done to you. Not only will your divorce be compelling to the judge, the judge will find you, personally, to be sympathetic, endearing, a candidate for sainthood for all you've put up with and the grace with which you've conducted yourself.

That is not how your day in court works.

YOUR DAY IN COURT

A multitude of factors make it difficult and unwise to trust your divorce to the final decisions of a single judge unless you absolutely have to.

First, judges typically have very little leeway in what rulings or remedies they can offer you. Judges are constrained by law, whereas two attorneys working for the best outcome in your particular circumstances can fashion creative ideas that might really help you and your family. Judges can and must do only what the law says they can and must do.

Judges have to rely on pertinent facts, which will not necessarily be the facts that are the most meaningful to you. Your attorney will probably have to deliver a pre-trial statement outlining the issues and your position on the issues. It's up to your attorney to sift through the mountains of information and documentation in order to make it as simple as possible for the judge.

As just one example, in some states child support ends before a child goes to college, and the court has no authority to make orders about payment of college or who supports the kids in college. This is a big issue for families, and it's possible to reach a settlement agreement that serves your children well during their college years. But without a settlement, in these states the judge can do nothing on this issue.

Some states also determine spousal maintenance, what used to be called alimony, using a very specific calculation. The same applies to most child support cases. The court plugs numbers into formulas and out pops the conclusion. In those states, even though fairness might clearly indicate that a person or child may be entitled to more or less, the courts can't grant what may morally or ethically be deserved. Judges can't always fashion the best awards because they have to follow the criteria they're given.

A settlement, on the other hand, can cover unexpected twists and turns in the future, as well as unique variables, like disability or the need to retool for the job market or a cash upfront settlement in lieu of spousal maintenance, so a spouse can buy a house or make a clean break from future obligations.

Also, you don't get to tell the judge which issues are most important to you; the ones you most hope to "win." The judge can't prioritize your issues the way you and your attorney can during mediation or negotiation.

Another drawback to having your day in court is the limited amount of time you'll have to tell your story to the judge. In many jurisdictions, you may have as little as one day to tell the story of a 30-year marriage. That means you may have only a few hours for your attorney to conduct direct examination of you and any witnesses you have, submit exhibits, conduct re-examination of you and your witnesses after the other side cross-examines you, and conduct cross-examination of the other side's witnesses. There's almost no ability to tell everything you want that judge to know, so you have to hit the most important parts. In fact, some of the things you think are very important may not even be admissible as evidence. It usually doesn't matter from a legal standpoint if your spouse had an affair, so the judge may never know what a lying, cheating scoundrel your STBX was, or that your STBX never went to church with you or made every trip to visit your family a miserable experience.

From a time standpoint, you don't get to talk at length. People forget that, in a courtroom, you don't have the opportunity to sit in front of a judge and bare your soul. You can only answer the questions that are asked and you may not be allowed to elaborate on some of the facts you really want to air. Especially when your

Overreaching

Krissy and David had been married only three years. He was the CEO of a large company; she headed up a large marketing company. When their daughter came along halfway into their marriage, they agreed Krissy would be a stay-at-home mom.

Because of her former career in a lucrative field, and the fact that she had not been out of the job market for long, the courts would not award Krissy as much spousal maintenance as she wanted. But no matter how many times I told her she would not receive the amount she had in mind, Krissy could not conceive of a judge giving her less. I recommended she settle. She would not let go of the number in her head.

So we went to court. In addition to the added costs of litigation, Krissy received less than she requested at court and even less than her STBX had agreed to in the settlement.

People believe if they overreach during negotiations, they'll receive something in the middle. And of course it's true that you shouldn't put your bottom line on the table first. But you shouldn't overreach so much that it offends the other side, or makes it appear you are so unreasonable that you can't be negotiated with. Judges tend to see it that way, too. By the time you get to trial, you may well lose if you have unreasonable expectations, and your unreasonableness may mean you end up getting slammed on everything else by the judge.

STBX's attorney objects and cross examines you. It's all time-consuming, and the time is limited.

Let's talk about your cross-examination. Your attorney will have elicited from you during your direct examination testimony all the good information you want the judge to hear. On your cross-examination the attorney for your STBX will focus on every shred of bad evidence that exists, and make you answer their questions yes or no, even if the question results in an answer that has been taken way out of context. If there is something bad out there, your attorney can help shield its blow by discussing it during your direct examination. And they get to ask you follow-up questions after your cross-examination.

Being grilled by your STBX's attorney is not going to be fun. It doesn't go the way you envision it before you get to court. Cross-examination is designed to make the judge see the cracks in your case.

When the trial is over, the animosity between you and your STBX will have been ratcheted even higher. Judges very rarely tell you their decision in court at the end of a trial, so neither you nor your attorney will know what you won or what you lost until the judge releases the written ruling—which could be days or weeks or months after your trial date.

Are you having fun yet?

Your best bet for achieving your personal goals is to settle on terms before you get to court. Use mediation. Use the collaborative model. Use whatever creative settlement options your attorney recommends, as long as they're legal, ethical, and result in positive outcomes for your divorced family.

ROLLING THE DICE

People hold onto the naïve belief that righteousness will be done. While there are very good judges, there are also very bad judges. Even very good judges sometimes get it wrong, even if they don't mean to. This is why we have courts of appeals and supreme courts.

One reason is that even the best judges can't set aside all their personal biases and life experiences in the process of applying the law to circumstances that leave so much room for personal interpretation. Or maybe the law in your state is not clear on how your dispute should be resolved, and both you and your STBX have valid points. The judge then just has to use his or her best discretion to reach an outcome—which may not be the outcome you sought. Remember, all the facts have to be boiled down to a limited amount. The facts that are in play have been interpreted by two different attorneys from two different perspectives. How a judge reacts to you is impacted by the tone of your case, which includes everything from the kinds of motions and documents your attorney files to the expression on your face when you sit in court.

The fact that going to court is a role of the dice is evidenced by an attorney education seminar held annually in our state. A mock trial is held before a panel of judges. At the end, all members of the judges' panel are asked how they would rule if the case was in front of them. Rarely are their rulings exactly the same, and rarely do they agree on what was most important in the evidence presented. Not because any of them are bad judges, but because they all come from different viewpoints and experiences.

What are some of the perspectives or biases an individual judge might bring to your case?

Judges don't like cases that are built on pointing fingers at other people, saying they're bad.

When the Judge Gets It Wrong

Stephanie and James looked like a fairy tale couple. She was beautiful and a successful professional. He came from old money, and a lot of it.

Even before Stephanie left her career to marry James, there were signs of trouble. She has letters he wrote apologizing for spoiling their time together with his anger. She even left him at the reception the night they married because his anger got out of hand.

During the marriage, James began to isolate her and cut her off from family and friends. After they had children, their older daughter even saw James' physical abuse of Stephanie.

During their long divorce litigation, before we got to trial, James was spending significant time with the children. But the children were beginning to balk about spending time with him. The older ones were still mad about the abuse they had seen against their mom. One child was even writing notes about wanting to die. One day, a confrontation at a parenting exchange resulted in James' arrest for assaulting Stephanie.

The court decided that the two older children, who had been impacted by the abuse, did not have to spend time with their father. However, the court decided that the youngest of the three children had not been impacted and could therefore continue to spend time with James, despite an expert opinion stating that it was likely just a matter of time before the youngest child was also damaged emotionally.

More than a year later, that ruling got tossed out the window because, in fact, the youngest of the three children had now been negatively impacted by the STBX's rage. The courts got it wrong, and this child paid the price.

Setting things right took time, cost more money and took a toll on a child.

WISING UP: Divorced families may have to return to court to change the terms of the divorce, especially when the judge gets it wrong, which costs more money, time and emotional stress. Knowing that, wouldn't you be wise to do everything you can to reach a settlement instead of leaving it up to the courts?

The Judge from Hell

When you're hoping for justice from that unbiased, wise, even-handed judge you imagine hearing your case, I want you to imagine instead the judge in one of my cases. He was so bad, I filed a complaint against him with our state's Judicial Commission on Ethics.

My client had reason to believe her STBX had been hiding a significant stream of income from a side business he was not reporting. We hired a private investigator who buddied up to him at a bar and got information that supported my client's contention. Our PI's testimony would prove my client was entitled to a better financial outcome than her husband was offering.

When we got to trial, the judge would not allow our PI to testify, a decision that was arbitrary and unfounded. Then my client got on the stand and the judge ripped into her—he was actually cross-examining her. It was clear to me that the judge didn't understand what her testimony was intending to convey, so I requested the opportunity to ask some follow-up questions. The judge refused my request.

At day's end, I requested more time to finish the trial. In a childish display of temper, the judge threw his pen onto his desk and stomped off the bench without ruling on my request. Stunned, we all waited. When the judge returned he said, "You can have more time. Come back on December 24."

I said, "Your honor, I won't be in town on December 24."

He said, "You're going to be here on December 24."

In all my years of practice, I had never seen a judge come across as so overtly antagonistic toward me or a client of mine. It was such a bad day that I filed a motion for the judge to recuse himself. He refused. Then I filed an emergency motion with the judge's superior to have the judge removed from the case. That resulted in a hearing. The outcome was that we got a new judge. But we had to start the trial all over.

This case had already been going on for more than a year. The new judge couldn't grant us a new trial for six months. At the new trial, my client ultimately got some of what she wanted, and the judge was fair. But redoing the trial cost her almost as much as she won. And it all turned on the arbitrary decisions and inappropriate behavior of a bad judge.

Judges have actually told me they assume whenever two people come into the courtroom for a divorce that they are both lying unless one party can prove he or she is telling the truth. Judges have typically been through more divorces than anyone else in the room and it's made them realistic, if not downright cynical.

Judges don't look kindly on what they view as unrealistic demands, whether made before a trial or at your trial. You and your attorney may consider it to be smart negotiating to ask for outrageous sums that no court will award or punitive custody terms designed to send a message to the STBX who has made your life hell. Or you may think it wise to overshoot your trial positions in order to get a ruling from the judge closer to what you really want.

Going too far in order to give yourself an edge in negotiations or at trial will not work to your advantage. What judges will see is greed or a complete inability to be reasonable or a total disregard for the children involved.

DECIDING YOUR LIFE

As you can see, your day in court has far more risk involved than you might imagine. It can be far less effective than you ever dreamed in giving you the wins that matter most to you.

A judge can fail to understand the facts or misapply the law, which can lead to an erroneous ruling. Or the judge may inadvertently forget to rule on one of the issues.

Even if you're very happy with the way the judge ruled, that may not be the end of it. There may be additional motions to file, issues that have been missed, rulings that were unclear, or an STBX who wants to appeal. Additional motion practice can go on for months. If either party actually appeals the judge's ruling, you may be divorced but could fight about the ruling for a year or more. The Court of Appeals may send the case back to the judge for a revised ruling or another hearing.

And going back to court for any reason means more litigation and more attorney fees.

That uncertainty is one reason it's a far better idea to settle out of court on as many issues as possible.

Also, don't discount the fact that people are more likely to abide by a ruling they've helped create and agreed to voluntarily than they are to stick with a decision handed down by a judge.

We put so much faith in the justice system and, in the case of divorces, in one individual to make determinations about the future. It's not just decisions about dollars, either. If you ask them to, judges are forced to decide your life.

Before you decide to give the courts that much control over you, ask yourself if there's any real logic in letting a person you have never met, whom will only see you for a few hours and whom you will probably never meet again decide the fate of your family, your finances, and your children.

Remember, we're looking for the Wiser Divorce—a divorce that results from a strategy to conclude your marriage by coming out the other side with a plan for creating your Next Best Life.

No judge can provide that. No judge will ask you what you really want out of life and nurture your goals and dreams. No judge is going to give you a hug when it's all over. Despite how learned and empathetic judges are, they must do the job they've been entrusted to do, within the boundaries of the law.

There are two sides to every story—even yours.

One final thing: Believe it or not, I've never seen a judge look down from the bench and say to the people in the court, "Let the record reflect that I've never seen such a clear-cut case of right and wrong!"

10   Plan Your Next Best Life

Remember Janet, my client in Chapter Two who made her dream of becoming a potter come true following her divorce at the age of 60?

Janet remains one of my most inspiring clients because of the way she embraced the opportunity to mold—literally and figuratively—a new life for herself. She owned responsibility for making herself happy in her Next Best Life.

You can do that, too.

No matter where you are, no matter what your circumstances are likely to be post-divorce, you can be like a potter, reshaping your life into what you want it to be.

Experiences like Janet's have taught me to ask the questions:

If you could have one dream job today, what would it be?

What have you always loved doing that you set aside to give more of yourself to your spouse or children?

What life goal did you think you would never achieve?

If your life is about to change, ask yourself the same questions. Then find someone to help you figure out what it would take to make that happen. Talk to someone who is doing what you dream about. Find out how much money it would take or what kind of training is necessary. This may be your opportunity to do something you've always wanted to do or go someplace you've always wanted to go or become involved in an activity you always wanted to try.

WISING UP: Your after-divorce life can look very different than your marriage life, physically, emotionally, or career-wise. Define the future you would like to live in and create a plan to make it happen.

A CONCRETE ACTION PLAN

As you make your journey through the process of transitioning from one stage of life to the next, you have a choice. You can hang onto the old patterns and the old hurts and drag them with you into your next stage of life. Or you can set your mind on making this a period of positive transformation.

Your Next Best Life Business Plan takes time and effort. Look at this process as an investment in yourself.

One of the keys to making it a positive transformation is to think strategically.

In business, the goal of strategic thinking is to turn your vision of the future into reality by developing and executing a concrete action plan. The same thing is true for your divorce. Without such a strategic plan, business gets messy. It gets inefficient and random, and business people end up in places they didn't expect, dealing with crises they never anticipated. They fail, sometimes in the same ways they failed in the past.

It happens because those business people didn't have a vision supported by a plan.

The best way to predict your future is to create it. So unless you want the next stage of your life to end up in another messy crisis, it's time to make your Next Best Life Strategic Plan.

GETTING REAL WITH YOURSELF

The steps in creating your personal Next Best Life plan are no different from the steps an entrepreneur would take in creating a business plan.

- Profit and Loss (P&L) statement
- Vision
- Goals
- Actions

You'll find Next Best Life planning documents in the appendix at the back of this book and on my website: AngieHallier.com. But here's a rundown of what it looks like and how you can use it.

Asset and Debt Inventory: Prepare a snapshot of your assets and debts. This will help you identify the financial issues that must be addressed in your divorce. It will assist your attorney in understanding your overall financial picture, identifying what documents may be needed, and what valuations may need to be performed.

Profit and Loss Statements for you and your children: Starting with your personal P&L gives you a clear snapshot of what you have to work with going forward—think of it as a personal inventory of your life at this point in time. When you first face the reality of divorce, everything can look like a loss. Lost years, lost dreams, lost security, lost confidence and more. Acknowledging and even cataloging those losses is important. Creating a good divorce doesn't mean living in denial. It means, among other things, getting real with yourself. That begins with listing all the positive things you're taking away from your divorce—your profits and gains—as well as the things that go in the debit column—your losses. When it comes to your children, think about how their lives have been, how divorce may change what they've known, and how you can facilitate a happy and healthy transaction for their own continued Next Best Life.

WISING UP: Once you've tallied the profits and losses, you are well-equipped to focus on the upside.

One practical advantage of working on the economic piece of your P&L is that it will begin to reveal what information you need in order to make wise decisions during settlement negotiations.

Vision: The view from Divorce Hell can be limited. Seeing beyond the dark horizon that's right in front of your nose won't be easy. In a way that's good because it can keep you from writing a fairy tale about your next life stage. A vision isn't a fairy tale. A vision is about hopes and dreams grounded in reality. With a new world opening up in front of you, where would you like to see yourself in a year, in five years, in ten years? How can you best plan for your children to maximize their own gains and minimize their losses? It's okay to look forward to a future that takes into account both your marital profits and losses and creates something new and positive.

Goals: With your vision taking shape, it's time to clearly articulate the specific outcomes you want to see for yourself and your divorced family. What are some big-picture goals that will begin to make your vision take shape? Professional goals—new career, additional training, developing long-ignored talents, blue-sky success markers for your current business. Personal goals—getting healthier, renewing friendships, strengthening family bonds, travel, hobbies, home ownership. Or goals for your children—staying in the same schools, never seeing you and your STBX argue—whatever you envision to keep your children emotionally healthy and happy. A goal is quantifiable and concrete.

Actions: Each goal is supported by specific actions, with timelines and success markers and the resources you need to succeed in those actions.

You can see that your Best Life Plan leads you from fear in your current state to a very real pathway for turning hopes and dreams into reality.

ASSETS FOR YOUR NEW LIFE

As you begin to work on your Profit and Loss Statements, you might want to concentrate on three key components of your life: Money, relationships, and personal satisfaction.

Money always plays a major role in a divorce. Who gets the house, the retirement funds, the savings account, the other assets that either add up to financial stability or point the way to reduced circumstances? Begin to inventory the major assets that will be divided during your divorce. By looking realistically at the financial assets, you'll be better prepared for a conversation with your attorney—and for developing realistic expectations about what may wind up in the financial columns of your personal P&L statement.

Will you stay in the house? Would you even want to, considering the financial implications of keeping it? How much will your current lifestyle suffer, especially if you have been a stay-at-home parent for much of your married life? How much of your hard-earned income will go for child support or spousal maintenance after the divorce? We've all seen the statistics about changes in economic status, post-divorce. How is that likely to impact you?

And how much liquid cash does the family have, pre-divorce? How much of that may end up in the "loss" column because of the cost of divorcing, especially if you decide to litigate instead of collaborate?

You can see how a realistic P&L statement could have an immediate positive impact on the direction your divorce negotiations take. Imagine the difference between leaving one-third of

◇◇

Grow Your Gains and Forget Your Losses

Identifying the marital gains you can grow and the losses you can leave behind can be tough, especially in the midst of the roller coaster of divorce. Here are a few ideas to jump-start your thinking. Can you add some of these things to your profit column?

- Less stress, less turmoil, less indecision.

- Less reliance on addictive substances or behaviors (alcohol, spending, gambling, eating, for example) to relieve depression or give you a shot of temporary happiness.

- Ways you can still depend on your STBX, especially if you have children.

- Things you still like about your STBX or learned from your STBX.

- More time with people who feed your spirit.

- Things you won't miss about being married (even the petty irritations that can add up to big irritants count here).

- More time to take care of yourself (exercise, eating healthy, sleeping better, for example).

- Positive life experiences, such as travel, the development of new parenting skills, exposure to different interests, hobbies or knowledge.

- Being clear about what a healthy relationship will or won't look like going forward.

your liquid resources in your attorneys' pockets, versus one-fourth or one-fifth or one-tenth. It can be the difference between stability and severely reduced circumstances for you and your children.

The next section of your P&L statement has to do with relationships—family, friends and, especially, your children.

Emotional intimacy is a big loss on your P&L statement. The positive spin on this loss is that the emotional intimacy is not a casualty of the divorce; more than likely, this loss had already occurred, or you wouldn't be in the middle of a divorce. Divorcing becomes your opportunity to find ways to bring emotional intimacy back into your life in the future.

What profits will you walk away with? If you and your STBX have children, certainly they are at the top of the profit side of your P&L equation. Maybe even in-laws or friends your STBX brought into your life may remain in the profit column—if you can divorce without rancor and name-calling and choosing sides. When collaborative divorce and mediation really work, even STBXs can become staunch allies and friends you can count on going forward. All those can go in the profit column.

Of course, if we make different choices, any of those relationships can also go in the loss column. If you try to play divide and conquer with friends and family, or your STBX does, certainly some will remain in your profit column and others will move into the loss column, as will the person you once chose as a life partner.

Even your relationship with your children is at risk during a divorce—and much of it depends on how you conduct yourself and how much you commit to putting your children first. Yes, there will be some losses. Family holidays and vacations won't be the same. You may miss being present for some key milestones in your children's lives, depending on how parenting time is handled. And certainly days and hours with your children will be lost, no matter how parenting time plays out.

Working through your P&L statements will begin to reveal how your actions and attitudes during the divorce process will ultimately impact your relationships, just as your economics can be impacted for good or bad. You'll finish the process understanding how to preserve more relationship capital in the profit column.

Your personal satisfaction columns will be a bit more subjective, harder to quantify, maybe. And certainly it may be harder to fill the profit column in the early stages of accepting divorce as your new reality. But I encourage you to dig deep here because the profits can be substantial if you're open to seeing them.

For your losses column, you'll certainly be looking at the loss of dreams. If you've always envisioned yourself sitting on the porch in a rocking chair, holding hands with your STBX and watching the grandchildren play during your golden years, you have a very real loss to face. How significant is the emotional toll you will have to recover from because of this divorce? What hits have your self-esteem, your personal confidence, your positive outlook on life taken?

Some losses are painful, but you know the pain will diminish. Other losses challenge your future happiness. It's the difference between a bruise and a broken leg. Know the difference and don't waste time agonizing over the first while ignoring the other, which needs your attention.

The profit column can feel elusive. You'll find more details to help you with this in the appendix, but for now, think about new opportunities for freedom, new adventures and experiences that might not have been possible during your marriage. Don't forget to tally up any emotional maturity or wisdom you may have gained during the years of your marriage. These are assets you will take with you into your new life. Acknowledge them, embrace them and celebrate them.

P&L statements also often take a look at risk. What risks do you face from divorce? Plan to talk with your attorney about how to mitigate the risks.

- Impacting your children's lives.

- Giving up something that is a high priority for you.

- Letting a judge decide the outcome.

- Spending so much money on the divorce that you can't fund your Next Best Life.

When I was going through my own divorce several decades ago, I kept reminding myself that because of the marriage I had been able to leave my parents' house and learn to stand on my own two feet. Yes, I was now a young single mom trying to forge a new career from scratch. But what I was taking away from the wreckage of that marriage was the strength and trust in myself to accomplish whatever I set out to do. I also learned what characteristics of a mate I never wanted to live with again.

Those are major assets for a young woman in her twenties. I learned to celebrate them, and I am well aware today that the years in that marriage contributed to my ability to achieve the success I have today and my work with others who are trying to regain their emotional well-being during the divorce process.

If you dig deep, I can just about promise that you'll find similar assets as you walk away from your marriage. If you don't name them and embrace them, you may squander them the way people squander money when they don't realize how hard-earned that money was. If you do acknowledge these personal assets, they are the building blocks for your Next Best Life.

FREE TO CREATE YOUR OWN LIFE

With a clear picture of where you are now, you can turn your attention to where you want to go—your vision for your future.

Although creating a vision for the future should be a positive thing, it's important to acknowledge that doing so can be tough when you're consumed by pain, uncertainty and fear. Drawing strength, encouragement and hope from the things listed in your profit column will help you as you try to imagine a new future while still sitting amid the ashes of a very recent past.

One of the best places to start may be with an honest look at the ways the marriage has either held you back or been significantly unfulfilling for you. Those areas represent your greatest opportunities for a wonderful new life.

Ask yourself these questions to get started:

- What dream (or dreams) did I set aside during this marriage? How might I jump-start that dream?

- How have the lives of my children been hindered by problems in the marriage? How can I and my STBX create conditions that will allow our children to flourish by cleaning up our personal issues?

- Who am I at my core—my passions, my purpose, my gifts and talents—and how can I embrace them more fully once I am single?

- What am I hungry for? How can I feed that hunger in positive ways now that I am free to create my own life?

Once you've let go of the old dreams that did not work, you'll find your new vision for your Next Best Life becomes your lifeline during the inevitable challenges of the divorce process.

BUILD ON A STRONG FOUNDATION

Out of your vision grow goals and from your goals you develop action steps.

Your goals are specific actions for turning your vision into reality. You may have a new career goal. If so, you'll develop the action plan for getting there, which may include additional training or education, or reconnecting with people in your network who can mentor or advise you. You may have new health or fitness goals, with an action plan for losing weight, getting in shape, getting your diabetes under control. You may have a goal of rebuilding a college fund for your children that was depleted because of the divorce. Maybe you have a goal of a new home where you can start fresh, with all the specific action steps necessary to make that happen.

It can be tempting to jump straight to actions you want to take. When that happens, the actions may not be strategic and can actually result in setbacks.

Here's an example: Finding a new relationship may sound like a great action plan if you haven't stepped back to gain perspective on where you are now and where you want to go. We've all heard about the dangers of rebound relationships, and one of the reasons they can be disasters is that they are built on the ruins of the old life instead of being built on a strong foundation of a vision for a Next Best Life.

Other quick-fix actions—buying a new car, moving across the country to get away from it all, selling the only house your children have ever known because you feel you can't stand to live there another day—can wind up being economic or emotional disasters.

Don't launch into action until you've taken an inventory and imagined your best new life.

GIVE YOURSELF A GIFT

Run this process. It gives you time and breathing room to shift into a strategic zone. It allows you to reflect and gain perspective from the relative safety of that strategic zone. It reminds you what really matters. It focuses your attention and energy on your children or your own healthy, happy future.

In other words, when you build a strategy for achieving your own Next Best Life, you are giving yourself a chance to achieve a Wiser Divorce. Give yourself this gift. It pays off now. It will pay off every day for the rest of your life.

That's the Wiser Divorce.

Transition Successfully

On the wall in my firm's offices is a framed newspaper story for which we were interviewed. The husband and wife in the story divorced when she realized she needed to live authentically as a lesbian. This couple had three children. They wanted to minimize the damage and disruption. After the divorce, the husband remarried, adding a wife and two other children to the picture. The first wife also had a new partner.

Today, they are a happy divorced family made up of three women, a man and five children. They celebrate holidays and birthdays and other life-affirming events as a family. The children truly are a blended family, hanging out together and forging bonds as siblings, as well as friends. Everyone in the family—moms, dad and children—go to therapy together, committed to continued healthy emotional growth and an expanded sense of what makes a family.

This inspiring family represents a new model, a divorced family that focused on making a successful life transition. They refused to craft a story that was about winners versus losers. As a result, they are all winners. Their lives are significantly richer than they had been before.

SHIFTING THE DIALOGUE

The fact that you're looking at this book probably means that your personal chances of experiencing divorce are high. You see it on the horizon, and your chance of avoiding it may be slim.

Just as divorce may be a fact in your life, it is a fact of modern life. By changing our thoughts, our words and our actions, we can change the way we view divorce. This will change the way we experience divorce and the way divorce impacts our lives. I know this to be true. When people change their thinking about divorce, from the notion of failure and animosity to an approach that is collaborative and healing, I've seen positive outcomes more times than I can count.

When we bring healthy, positive thoughts, words, and actions to the table, we can make a successful transition to our Next Best Life. We can do that one divorcing family at a time.

Unless we eliminate divorce—and the chances of that happening are slim to none and would not, in my opinion, be a healthy step for many families anyway—we must eliminate the attitudes that make divorce such an overwhelmingly negative experience. By shifting the dialogue about divorce, we can eradicate the stigma that beats down families and adds to the emotional disruption. By shifting the dialogue about divorce, we can reincarnate the divorced family as a richer, healed relationship that supports children and adults emotionally and economically.

We can turn a divorce into an event that allows people to transition from a version of life that is not working into their Next Best Life.

FORGIVENESS AND HEALING

Sometimes, our best selves show up and triumph even in the middle of a very unpleasant divorce. Sometimes, people gain something far more valuable than they imagined when they walked into a settlement negotiation.

One of the best days of my career came when I was a settlement officer between Alan and Gina, a couple who had been married almost 25 years. They moved to Alan's farm, which had been in his family for generations, despite the fact that Gina was a confirmed city dweller who wasn't sure how she felt about all those farm animals and open spaces. Alan convinced her that the family farm would be a perfect place to raise a family and she agreed to try it.

During those 25 years, Gina and Alan had two children, a son and a daughter who were both now away at college. In addition, Gina surprised everyone by falling in love with life on the farm. She loved gardening and became active in the organic food movement. She wrapped her life around their two children and farm living.

When the marriage fell apart, Alan decided it was the perfect time to get rid of the farm that had been in his family for generations. He resented the fact that it now felt more like Gina's farm than his. He also believed that since their children had left for school, their attachment to the farm would also diminish. When he announced his intention, however, the children surprised him. They announced that they wanted to move back to the farm to live with their mother and attend a local college during the divorce.

Alan resented this attachment to Gina and refused to budge.

This made their son and daughter furious; both of them tried repeatedly to talk him into letting their mother Gina stay on the farm, so they could one day inherit it and continue the family tradition. Alan refused, largely because he saw that Gina was more a part of his children's family tradition than he was.

When it was time to negotiate the settlement, these young adult children came to support their mother.

Alan felt so angry over what felt like his children's betrayal that he wouldn't speak to them. The son and daughter didn't even want to be in the same room with their father.

I realized I would have to talk to each party separately in different rooms. After talking to Gina and the children, I looked Alan in the eye and said, "I need you to think about the most graceful way you can exit this marriage. I want you to think about how this woman embraced your family's heritage and passed in down to another generation. I want you to decide if you really want to be the instrument of destroying that family legacy and the generations of connection it has created for them."

After some thought, Alan decided to back down. In the end, he agreed to allow Gina to remain on the farm as long as she wanted, with the understanding that the farm would be passed to their children.

When I explained his decision to Gina and the children, they all started crying. The daughter said, "Mom, this means he realizes that we are who we are because of you and the way you kept family traditions alive."

When I told Alan they were all crying because they appreciated what he had done, he got teary-eyed, too. Then they all came together, and hugged and cried together.

Even in the middle of this inevitable divorce, forgiveness and healing occurred because they were able to acknowledge that who owned a piece of property was far less important than healing.

REACH FOR THE WISER DIVORCE

Your part, of course, is to plan your divorce as an affirmative action instead of allowing the process to happen to you or to victimize you. Your part is to walk through it with the awareness that it should carry no more stigma than a business partnership that ends.

Normalize your own divorce. Let it show in your interactions with friends, family, your STBX, and particularly in your choice of attorneys and the process you choose to follow in divorcing. Walk through it with wisdom.

My wish for you, if divorce is inevitable, is that you divorce gracefully and find positive transformation in building your Next Best Life.

That is the Wiser Divorce.

NEXT BEST LIFE WORKSHEETS

The following pages show samples of four Next Best Life planning worksheets that can be downloaded at AngieHallier.com and printed full size.

PROFIT AND LOSS STATEMENT: MONEY*

ASSET	VALUE	WHAT YOU'D LIKE TO DO WITH IT	WHAT THE LAW SAYS SHOULD BE DONE WITH IT
1. Real property			
2. Bank accounts			
3. Retirement plans			
4. Investments			
5. Insurance policies			
6. Business interests			
7. Inheritance			
8. Vehicles			
9. Furnishings, art and other personal belongings			

DEBT	AMOUNT	WHAT YOU'D LIKE TO DO WITH IT	WHAT THE LAW SAYS SHOULD BE DONE WITH IT

*This is not a substitution for your after-divorce budget. Before you can make final decisions about your assets and debts, you must also understand what your after-divorce budget will or should look like, both before and after taxes.

PROFIT AND LOSS PERSONAL SATISFACTION

CATEGORY IDEAS	GAINS (What you love that got pushed aside during your marriage that you want to regain)	LOSE IT AND FORGET IT (The bad in the marriage you won't carry forward)	NEW BEST LIFE (Goals and desired outcomes)	ACTION STEPS FOR YOUR GOALS
1. Exercise & health				
2. Personal care: Hair, massages, clothing, etc.				
3. At home life: Schedule, food, pets, decorations, and furnishings				
4. Communication				
5. Food: Cooking, where you eat, what you eat				
6. Activities & hobbies				
7. Talents				
8. Learning/Education/Training				
9. Security: Financial or otherwise				
10. Spirituality				

PROFIT AND LOSS PERSONAL SATISFACTION *(continued)*

11. Indulgences				
12. Passions/Dreams/Purpose/Gifts				
13. Discretionary spending/Savings				
14. Travel				
15. Career/Profession				
16. Family bonds/Friends				
17. Emotional: Confidence, conflict, stress, maturity, wisdom, intimacy				
18.				
19.				
20.				
21.				
22.				

PROFIT AND LOSS STATEMENT: CHILDREN

CATEGORY IDEAS	HOW IT WAS IN MARRIAGE (The family structure your children have experienced until now)	REALITY (Possible changes from divorce — positive or negative)	GOALS FOR YOUR CHILDREN (To keep them safe and happy)	ACTIONS (Steps to make your goals work for your children)
1. Health related needs: Doctors, dentists, eyeglasses, disabilities				
2. Property: Computers, games, toys, books				
3. Pets				
4. Spiritual/Religious				
5. Care providers				
6. Holidays				
7. Extended family				
8. Physical Needs: Scheduling, bathing, food, bedroom furnishings, clothing, haircuts, etc.				